to
→ WALLY

know
GNOTHI
SEAVTON

yourself
love
from
MAMMS + TATUS
CHRISTMAS
1997
♥

talks, stories,

and articles

on Zen

to
know
yourself

talks, stories,

and articles

on Zen

by Albert Low

Charles E. Tuttle Co., Inc.
Boston • Rutland, Vermont • Tokyo

First published in 1997 by Tuttle Publishing, an imprint of Periplus
Editions (HK) Ltd., with editorial offices at 153 Milk Street, Boston,
Massachusetts 02109.

The Library of Congress Catalog Card Number: 97–61461

Distributed by

USA
Charles E. Tuttle Co., Inc.
RR 1 Box 231-5
North Clarendon, VT 05759
Tel.: (800) 526-2778
Fax.: (800) FAX-TUTL

Japan
Tuttle Shokai Ltd.
1-21-13, Seki
Tama-ku, Kawasaki-shi
Kanagawa-ken 214, Japan
Tel.: (044) 833-0225
Fax.: (044) 822-0413

Southeast Asia
Berkeley Books Pte. Ltd.
5 Little Road #08-01
Singapore 536983
Tel.: (65) 280-3320
Fax.: (65) 280-6290

First edition
05 04 03 02 01   00 99 98 97   1 3 5 7 9 10 8 6 4 2

Design by Frances Kay
Cover design by Sherry Fatla

Printed in the United States of America

Dedicated to my brother and sister.

Contents

To practice Zen is to know the self.
To know the self is to forget the self.
To forget the self is to be one with all that is.
To be one with all things is to go beyond body and mind.
To go beyond body and mind is to go beyond awakening
while manifesting it at every moment.

Ackowledgments

*I should like to thank all the members of the Montreal Zen Center who have
helped me bring together this collection, and in particular, I thank Janine
Levêsque who has patiently transcribed the talks which have served as a
basis for several of the articles.*

Montreal, 1997

Preface

This book contains a collection of articles, talks, and stories that I have written, given, or used over the past seventeen years as teacher and director of the Montreal Zen Center. Some of these first appeared in the Montreal Zen Center magazine *Zen Gong*. These include: "Some Thoughts About Practice," "Know Yourself!," "The Mountain of Inertia," "Wonder of Wonder," "Fear of Failure," "On Pain," and "At Sea." A few of them, including "The Life of Buddha, the Life of Everyone," "Shrinking Zen," and "A Sesshin," were written during my three years' tenure as editor of the Rochester Zen Center magazine *Zen Bow,* and they are reproduced with the kind permission of the Rochester Zen Center. The three commentaries on the koans were originally given as talks during a retreat held in Montreal, but have been edited and enlarged. The style of presentation was considerably changed in order to make them more accessible to general readers outside the Montreal Zen Center, whose members have become used to the language of these kinds of talks.

PART 1

Articles

The Life of Buddha, the Life of Everyone

This is the story of a monk. It tells of why he became a monk, of the sufferings he endured, and of his great enlightenment. Although this monk lived twenty-five hundred years ago, this story is not simply history. If it were so, it would have no relevance to those who are caught up by the most vital of questions.

Let us tell the story first and then see how it can be shown to go far beyond the mere tale of a man long dead.

Twenty-five hundred years ago a child was born, the son of a king in India. At his birth the wise men foretold that he would grow up to become either a king or a monk. His father, not wanting his son to have to endure the hardship of an ascetic's life and also wanting to ensure the continuance of his line, shielded the child from the troubles of life and gave him all the security and pleasures that money could buy.

The child, called Siddhartha Gautama, grew up to be an accomplished man, capable in the arts and sciences of his time. In due course he married and had a child. But he grew restless and felt bound by the pleasures his father lavished upon him and wanted to see more of life than that enclosed by the walls of the villas in which he lived. He summoned his charioteer and rode into the rough-and-tumble world of the common man, and in that world he encountered a sick man, an old man, and a dead man.

He was confounded by the encounters and asked his charioteer to explain their meaning. He was told that this was

3

the lot of all and that none could escape these three: sickness, old age, and death. His mind foundered in a turmoil, but confused and lost, he had yet one more encounter—this time with a monk. Inspired by the deep serenity and peace of mind pervading this man, Gautama vowed he too would become a monk.

One night, bidding farewell to his wife and child while they slept, he stole away into the forest to become a wandering ascetic, cutting off his hair, symbolizing the severance of all worldly ties. He studied with the forest sages but, after learning all they had to offer, still felt dissatisfied and without rest. He traveled on and met some ascetics and, joining them, practiced all the ascetic trials. He starved himself and inflicted many different kinds of torment on his person. In the end and near to death, he remembered a time when he watched his father and the workers plow. At that time he had become one with all the strain and suffering of the world. Remembering this experience and how it had seemed to open the door to a deep awareness of unity, he resolved to give up his ascetic practice, which could only lead to death, and seek to reawaken to this Oneness.

At that very moment a girl, Nandabala the cowherd, was passing by and, seeing Gautama weak through lack of food, gave him some goat's milk to drink. Revived, Siddhartha then went on, in search of a suitable place to meditate. He came upon the Bo tree. Sotthiya, a grass cutter passing by, gave him some grass on which to sit. Gautama took the grass and spread it under the tree. Then, taking his seat, he vowed, "Though my flesh wither and drop from my bones, though my bones be crushed, though my blood dry up and turn to dust, never will I stir from this seat until I reach full enlightenment." Then, throughout the long night he was tempted by Mara. At dawn he looked up at the morning star; suddenly he became fully awakened and cried, "Wonder of wonders, all beings are endowed with Buddha-nature."

How are we to interpret this story? As a historical or biographical account of a monk's life? Or does it have some other value? Siddhartha Gautama, who became Shakyamuni Buddha, was undoubtedly a most remarkable man. Alone he brought

4

about a great spiritual revival that was to transform parts of India, Tibet, China, Southeast Asia, Korea, Japan—and now, who knows, perhaps North America also. Even after twenty-five hundred years his teachings are still vital and, many would say, the only valid way for us to find a path through our technological stupor to find wholeness and meaning. The life story of such a great man would be interesting, full of drama, and perhaps even inspiring. It could make a great subject for research and study. But in the end, if that is all it is—the story of a great man—would it not have but very limited value?

The great and fundamental teaching of Buddhism is that all is One—there is no Other. Oneness is the goal, the means, and the consequence. In Oneness we start the journey, in Oneness we continue, and in Oneness we end. Undivided, forever at home, we are nevertheless captivated by the illusions that rise out of the waves of the mind, and in this captivation our Oneness is seemingly shattered as the reflection of the moon is scattered and spread on the surface of a pond disturbed by the wind.

Buddha's last words to his closest disciples were as follows:

"Be islands unto yourselves, be a refuge to yourselves; do not take to yourselves any other refuge. See truth as an island, see truth as a refuge. Do not seek refuge in anyone but yourselves."

It is by becoming a refuge to oneself, by not seeking truth outside, and by letting go of the mirage of the Other that the winds die down and wholeness becomes apparent, and the shattering is seen as an illusion.

As such, the simple life story of a great man, it is of little value. Indeed, however great his truth and wise his teachings, if he is exalted and worshipped, this in itself could become the greatest and most impenetrable barrier blocking out forever the very freedom that he strove so hard to make known to us. To seek to "imitate" Buddha, to try to be "like" Buddha, would be like cutting off your feet while learning to walk or like putting out your eyes while trying to see. Raising Buddha up on a pedestal, seeing him as unique among men, incomparable,

unapproachable, otherworldly, is to open a chasm of unfath-
omable depths in the very ground upon which you stand.
Religion is considered by many to be a harbor or refuge to
shield one from the storms of life. A great Bach cantata rings
out in triumph: "A mighty fortress is our God." But this is not
the way of Zen. Every harbor eventually becomes a stagnant
backwater, every fortress a prison.

With this in mind one may well ask, What then is the
value of this life of Shakyamuni? Zen master Mumon said, "You
who realize enlightenment will be able to say, 'Were the honored Shakyamuni and the great Bodhidharma to appear, I
would cut them down instantly, demanding, Why do you totter
forth? You are no longer needed.' " With such an ultimate aim
in view, why worry about this story?

It is because the life of Gautama is the life of Everyman, of
you and me, whether man or woman. In this lies its great inspiration.

*Twenty-five hundred years ago a child was born, the son of a
king in India.*

Both the Lotus Sutra of Buddhism and the New Testament
of Christianity tell the same parable. It reads roughly as follows:
There was once a son of a king who left home and wandered far
away. In wandering, he gradually lost all but the faintest memory of his origins. He fell on hard times and became a beggar.
To support himself, he looked after pigs that belonged to
another, sharing the acorns and husks they were given to eat.
The day came when, out of the very depths of his despair and
misery, the memory of who and what he was suddenly revived
and became a compelling force in his life. He left the sties and
returned home to his father.

Each of us is the son or daughter of a king, and each is
heir to a kingdom, which is no less than the whole universe
itself. The king is the true nature of each of us and each of us
wanders far from our true home. Our true nature is our
Buddha-nature. *Buddha* means "awakened" and implies "knowing" in itself. Because there is no "other," because "from the very
beginning of things" we do not basically know "something,"

because knowing and being are not separate, there is nothing to know and nothing that knows. Because this is so, all is contained in knowing and nothing lies outside: we are whole and complete, this very mind is Buddha. The whole world is a kingdom, and the whole world is king.

At his birth wise men foretold that he would grow up to become either a king or a monk.

We are not one, we are two; although these two are like the two faces of a coin, which is one whole. At birth we have the potential to be a king or a monk, and the basic struggle and war that tears us throughout our lives is between these two faces. When we reach out to conquer, to act in the world, something within seems denied. When we turn inward seeking truth and reality, we feel the waste of passing time; we get restless. We reach a point where no matter what we do, we feel we should be doing something else. One of the most pervasive and poignant feelings that floods many is that somehow life is passing them by. Those who are caught up in life's affairs often yearn after a world of solitude, of peace and tranquillity. Those who live withdrawn from the world often long for action and busyness. While the king stalks and storms across new realms of being, the monk lies distraught, shriveled through lack of food and sunlight; while the monk penetrates ever deeper into the realm of knowledge and wonder, the king languishes limp and spineless, his vigor spent, his adventurous spirit timorous and hesitant. It is as though at our birth we are mortally wounded.

His father, not wanting his son to have to endure the hardship of an ascetic's life and also wanting to ensure the continuance of his line . . .

This is the role that parents assume: the protectors. A baby is born; it is weak and helpless, but endowed by nature with one deadly weapon—the smile. We may live a rambling life, wandering dissolute and not caring too much about anything. We marry and then a baby is born. At first it is almost a vegetable—wet and cantankerous. But with its smile it holds hostage the whole life of mother and father. They work, labor, and suffer to maintain that smile. The smile that brings the whole world into one radiance. The smile of a baby is without guile or conceit, and through it we glimpse once more our awakened nature, our own life of oneness.

It is natural that Suddhodana, Gautama's father, should want to shield his son from a life of privation and asceticism. There is no suffering quite as hard to bear as the suffering of your own child. Your own suffering can be struggled with, seen through, used as a source of energy, transmuted. The suffering of your spouse is worse, but you can talk together, console, and encourage or together walk through the valley. But when your child lies there in pain, mute and patient though perplexed and afraid, what do you do? How to bring back the smile? It is said with truth that children are hostages to fortune. You worry that they may go astray, that they may get onto the wrong path, that they may end up doing the same foolish things, stumbling into the same ditches, and falling over the same rocks as you did yourself. "Your child will grow up to be successful, strong, admired by all, in a position of great power—or it may be a nothing, unknown, poor, ridiculed, and humiliated, searching for what the immortals themselves could never find." It is natural that Suddhodana should not want his son to be an ascetic.

[He] shielded the child from the troubles of life and gave him all the security and pleasures that money could buy.

This is the great tragedy: in the great love we have for our children, we deny them suffering. We lavish on them all that we can afford, and the children sooner or later grow up to hate us and accuse us of being phony. The trouble is that they are right: a life without acknowledged suffering—one that is lived in the pretense that pain and anxiety, humiliation, fear, despair and guilt, sickness and disease, injury and death, are accidents or the visitation of some malevolent force—is at best a half-life, half-death. We compound our fault by giving the children what they want, often to avoid the hassle that will follow if we don't. Our whole society is like this. We are like children who now turn and hate the parent who has provided drugs to protect us from the pains of life, has turned death into an unreal phantom, has provided us with ready-made Technicolor™ dreams in boxes that we can set up in a living room of soft plush furniture, has provided us with oranges and bananas in midwinter and honey all year round, has given us wheels to roll us and wings to fly us to beaches and sun and fun and sea. Indeed, we have all the pleasures money can buy. But we have learned to hate doctors, hate supermarkets, hate cars and airplanes, hate TV and cinema. The tragedy is that the tragedy is endless and enacted in the name of love.

The child, called Siddhartha Gautama, grew up to be an accomplished man, capable in the arts and sciences of his time.

One of the most common beliefs of those who do not practice a religion is that those who do are somehow incompetent. They are considered dropouts who seek religion as a solace, an escape from the hard facts of life, because they cannot cope. Undoubtedly there are many who do use religion as an escape. But do not many others likewise use work, sex, friendship—in fact, almost anything—as a shield against the pain of their lives? But because some do so, it does not mean that all do so. Because some use work to avoid facing their problems, it does not mean that all who work are workaholics. It is clear from the stories that have come down to us that Shakyamuni was not one who could not cope.

However, at the same time we must be careful not to make the mistake of believing that aptitudes and abilities as the world knows them are requirements for "progress" on the spiritual path or that they are the outcome of work upon oneself. Our skills and abilities are given to us—they unfold as the petals of a flower unfold. Sometimes the circumstances are right and everything flows, and we like to believe that we are the authors. At other times nothing goes right. We struggle and strain, work and toil, but nothing fits and everything keeps falling apart. Then we prefer to believe that we are victims of a fate over which we have no control.

In due course he married and had a child.

Thus, the round is now complete. Starting as a child, one becomes a parent. Starting as the protected, one becomes the protector. The wheel of life is inexorable; it goes around and we, caught up and enmeshed in that wheel, go around with it.

Some say that at his birth Buddha was aware that he had a great mission to fulfill and that his early life was lived in full consciousness of this mission. But the facts suggest otherwise. Gautama got married—he pursued the course of Everyman. He married for all the reasons that men and women marry, and when he married, he probably committed himself to the marriage believing that in this way he could reach final happiness.

It is a truth that is sometimes difficult to accept that wealth and contentment are quite unrelated to each other. "If only I had more money," "a different home," "a better job," "a more understanding spouse," "more clothes" . . . the list is endless. George Bernard Shaw is reputed to have said that the value of a university education is that it shows us nothing is lost by not having had one. The same could be said for all wealth. One can have plenty of money and still feel that one lacks; one can have a good job and still feel unchallenged; one can have a wonderful marriage with beautiful children and still be gnawed by loneliness; one can have considerable talent and still feel inferior. All of this we know. We have seen that time and again we have been taken in by the illusory promise of satisfaction, and yet still we are sucked in by the next dream we happen to fall victim to.

But he grew restless and felt bound by the pleasures his father lavished upon him and wanted to see more of life than that enclosed by the walls of the villas in which he lived.

This restlessness is like an itch that itches, which is the way one teacher put it. It is like the itching of chilblains—the more we scratch, the worse it gets. This restlessness is the precursor to the real search. In our very depths something stirs. We are amazed that everyone is not equally restless. Values that we once held dear, activities that we enjoyed, ideas that we flirted with, all turn to dust and ashes. The restlessness gets panicky, and we see things that we had overlooked before. They stare us in the eye, and we know that we cannot hide from them anymore. For the moment they are reality, while everything else is but flickering shadows.

It is said that if nature is thrown out the front door, she comes back in through the window. It is foolish to believe that we can shelter ourselves or others from the suffering of life. It is said that there was once a businessman who happened to hear that Yama—the god of death—was coming for him the next day. The man started to shake and perspire and wring his hands; he did not know what to do. Eventually he hit upon a solution. If Yama was coming for him, then he would not be there when Yama came. He would travel to a distant country and hide among the people there, and Yama would never find him. So he bought an airline ticket, boarded the plane, and soon found himself being pushed along in the crowds of the country to which he had fled. As he struggled in the crowd he looked up, and there coming toward him with a broad smile was Yama. "Ah! There you are," said Yama. "We have an appointment for today, and I was just wondering how I would ever get to your house in time. Now here you are!"

The best-laid schemes of mice and men often go awry, as the Scottish poet Robert Burns said. Not because there is anything inherently wrong with the plan. The mice that Burns came across in the field he was plowing had chosen the perfect spot for their nest and had built their nest with the greatest care. But there was another plan: the farmer wanted to harvest his crop, and in doing so he turned up the mice's nest and destroyed their plan.

Each of us is subject to our karma, that is, subject to the totality of forces that we set in motion moment by moment with every act, choice, and decision we make. Sometimes these forces are long in catching up, sometimes scarcely have we sown the seed than we are reaping the whirlwind. An inexorable law holds sway that is higher than any effort we may make on our own or another's behalf to subvert it. Everything has a cause, every cause has an effect.

He summoned his charioteer and rode into the rough-and-tumble world of the common man, and in that world he encountered a sick man, an old man, and a dead man.

Sickness, old age, and death—the inevitable lot of all people. How we try to shield ourselves from these specters! We like to believe that these are accidents that happen only to others. Sickness is an interruption in living, something we do not always have time for. Old age can be bought off with cosmetics, exercises, plans, and optimism. Death can be buried under elaborate rituals, expensive accessories, beautiful flowers. But still these three make themselves known—a twinge here, a sudden pain there, and we are staring down the red throat of Yama.

A new syndrome seems to be making itself known; it afflicts people typically at the age of forty. Sometimes later, sometimes earlier, but always it has the same components. The person feels completely at sea, without any support. All compensations seem to shrivel, and one is faced with death. One sees the inevitability of old age leading to death and dreads sickness, which will be the precursor of old age. Jung has said that the neurosis of the young person arises from the fear of life, but the neurosis of a person older than forty arises from the fear of death. Not all are affected by this syndrome, but wealth, power, skills, or vitality are no safeguard against it. About the age of forty many do foolish things: they give up secure jobs and start new careers, they divorce mates they have loved and lived with for years, they develop strange neuroses, some even drop dead. For years they have avoided an encounter with the apocalyptic trio by swift footwork, moving, bobbing and weaving; plans, goals, objectives, have mortgaged the future until they run out of time. . . .

Finally he met a wandering monk.

What an encounter that was! Had that monk not taken that route, how different might the history of the world have been. But that encounter was determined before time; it was Buddha's karma—our karma.

The most terrible suffering is useless suffering. The suffering of cows, horses, dogs, squirrels, elephants, crocodiles—this is terrible because it seems so useless. But suffering in human beings may be followed by an encounter with a monk, with a holy man, with a man who has given up everything in the certain knowledge that he can, and will, find the truth. Suffering prepares the way for that encounter; and provided the suffering is taken in, provided it is intentional, the encounter with the monk is inevitable because the monk is none other than the call of our true nature.

One night, bidding farewell to his wife and child while they slept, he stole away into the forest to become a wandering ascetic . . . .

This was the way it was done in India and is still done to this day. As an example of this, J. G. Bennett, the British mathematician and philosopher and student of Gurdjieff, has written of his encounter with Shivapuri Baba, an Indian ascetic, who died in the late 1950s at the age of 132. Shivapuri Baba left home at the age of eighteen and was in the forest for twenty-five years, alone, before coming to a great awakening. Incidentally, after his awakening he said that he rehabilitated himself into society and then at the age of sixty walked around the world and visited a great number of eminent people of the day.

Ramana Maharshi is another; at the age of seventeen and after a great awakening, he also left the home of his parents to travel to Mount Arunachala, where he remained for the rest of his life.

But stories such as these must be understood very carefully. It was not a question of abandoning wife and family or mother and father. Some people who misunderstand the intention and mind-state of Buddha wonder how an apparent act of irresponsibility could have a worthwhile outcome. The law of karma rules that from an evil action, evil will sooner or later flow. But Buddha's act was fully in accord with his karma. His wife and family were well cared for. People who wrestle and worry about leaving home or giving up a job or starting something new are most likely not ready for the move.

Other societies, particularly those with less hospitable climates, do not have this tradition of going into the forest and simply living off the earth. But it is not the fact of leaving home that is so important. It is the act of renunciation. To start seriously along a spiritual path, it is of fundamental importance that one "renounce the world." This can be done even though there is no obvious change in routine or activity. The act of renunciation is made when one sees unequivocally that the "world" and all that it stands for cannot assuage one iota the anguish of the spirit. One sees right through the world and for a while stands naked and alone. William James says that the religious path starts with a cry for help. The moment of renunciation can be a terrible moment, and one feels so powerless, so alone, that one cries out for some support. Try as one may, one cannot recant. Something is destroyed at that moment which can never be replaced. One must now go forward relentlessly or fall from the human scene.

He studied with the forest sages but, after learning all they had to offer, still felt dissatisfied and without rest.

His teachers were Alara Kalama, Rama, and Uddaka. The first, Alara, taught a way to reach the realm of the void, but no further. Rama took Buddha further to the realm where there is no more perception of anything, and Uddaka was able to take him further, but very little. The realm of the void and the realm where there is no perception are still in the realm of consciousness and form; they are still based upon *something* that knows the void or has gone beyond perception. No ultimate security comes from this. Many forms of meditation can take us out of ourselves, so to speak. Some require great discipline and effort. But liberation is only true liberation when it manifests in our everyday life. "What is truth?" someone asked Joshu. "When I'm hungry, I eat; when I'm tired, I sleep." Mind-states that are exalted, full of glory, light, and hosannas are but the peak of the roller coaster that in no time plunges to the bottom. Psychic states held tenuously in silence and isolation are simply mental gymnastics, and just as the practice of physical gymnastics does not bring ultimate peace, so mental pyrotechnics, ESP, levitation, and psychic states generally are of no value in leading us to the Great Liberation.

*He traveled on and met some ascetics and, joining them, prac-
ticed all the ascetic trials.*

How often does one see this: life is unsatisfactory, so some
ascetic practice is carried out; most frequently, some form of
fasting or breath control is undertaken. Gautama practiced for
six years and reached a point where he was eating but one grain
of rice each day. But there are degrees of asceticism, and
undoubtedly the stabs at dieting that so many undertake and
the jogging epidemic that has infected America are also but
ersatz ascetic practices carried out for lack of a true understanding of how to practice spiritual discipline.

Even *zazen* practiced outside the guidance of an experienced teacher can degenerate into a subtle form of asceticism.
There is the famous *mondo* between Nangaku and Baso:

Nangaku observed Baso practicing zazen and asked him
what he was doing. Baso replied that he was trying to become a
Buddha. Nangaku seized a tile and started to grind it on a rock.
This time it was Baso's turn to ask Nangaku what he was doing.
Nangaku said that he was polishing it to make a mirror.

"How should polishing a tile make it a mirror?" Baso
asked.

"How could sitting make a Buddha?" retorted Nangaku.

Baso then asked, "What should I do then?"

Nangaku replied, "If you were driving a cart and it wouldn't
go, would you whip the cart or the ox?"

Baso made no reply.

The point of the story is not—as some would believe—to
give up zazen but rather to give up using zazen as a form of
asceticism. In practicing asceticism, we simply tear at the twigs
and branches while the root flourishes all the more.

*In the end and near to death, he remembered a time when he
watched his father and the workers plow. At that time he had become
one with all the strain and suffering of the world.*

The enlightenment before enlightenment. The sudden
unbidden taste of freedom that settles for a moment, then flies
away like a startled bird. It is surprising how many people have
had this taste. It comes in all kinds of ways: in the evening on a

holiday, in listening to music, in falling in love, in a moment of intense grief, in sickness, in a moment of profound pity. It comes . . . and is gone. It is so familiar and yet breathtaking in its freshness. One looks through a crack in existence for a flash, but it is enough. The time will come when this encounter matures and, like a lodestone, acts as a guide, and more and more our tendencies turn in one direction until finally we are carried forward as if by an irresistible force, to seek awakening.

Remembering this experience and how it seemed to open the door to a deep awareness of unity, he resolved to give up his ascetic practice, which could only lead to death, and seek to reawaken to this Oneness.

This is a great moment. For Buddha once was enough; but others, as time and again they fall back from the truth, time and again must they reawaken to the uselessness of all their self-inflicted pains. With a touch of truth everything becomes so simple and obvious. One wonders how one could have gotten so thoroughly lost; but again and again we crash off into the tangled undergrowth of brambles and briars, blindly trying to force a way through to where there is no need to go. So often do we hear "give up your striving," "don't disturb the mind," "just put down your burden," but as often we adopt techniques and ways; we try this or push that, think this or do that. It is by letting go of everything, by the total sacrifice of all—even what we prize most, our practice of spiritual discipline—that our deepest intuition can be awakened and, through this awakening, the veil of duality pierced.

At that very moment a girl, Nandabala the cowherd, was passing by and, seeing Gautama weak through lack of food, gave him some goat's milk to drink. Revived, Siddhartha then went on, in search of a suitable place to meditate. He came upon the Bo tree. Sotthiya, a grass cutter passing by, gave him some grass on which to sit.

Roshi Kapleau in *The Three Pillars of Zen* writes, "You can rely on this: once you enter upon the Buddha's way with sincerity and zeal, Bodhisattvas will spring up everywhere to help you." So often it is the case that one no-mindedly resolves to liberate oneself, and then the help of others appears naturally and without effort. This is not an example of the power of positive thinking but quite the opposite. Once we have surrendered our willfulness and sacrificed our dearest barriers to awakening, we are open to the whole world—and in this state of oneness we naturally have what is necessary. *Bodhisattvas* are often considered in Buddhism to be exalted beings who are next only to Buddha himself. But in Zen a bodhisattva is the one who helps you along the path. Sometimes this help is obvious when it is meted out by a Zen teacher or someone who is advanced on the way. But sometimes it is not so obvious: the woman who crashes into your car, the bureaucrat who insists upon the right form, the policeman who gives you a ticket—these are no less bodhisattvas than the girl who gave you the book on Zen or than the man who told you about the workshop or than the fellow who gave you a lift to the Zen Center.

Then, taking his seat, he vowed, "Though my flesh wither and drop from my bones, though my bones be crushed, though my blood dry up and turn to dust, never will I stir from this seat until I reach full enlightenment."

One account goes on to say that "he sat himself down cross-legged in an unconquerable position, from which not even the descent of a hundred thunderbolts at once could have dislodged him." This is the supreme moment. With such resolve, what could go wrong? It was not only the body that was immovable but the mind also. Body/mind rocklike. Thoughts, like flies, dash against such resolve in vain. The whole world transparent. Even though one sits amid confusion and noise, nothing stirs, not even awareness that nothing stirs.

Then, throughout the long night he was tempted by Mara.

Mara is the evil one. The word *mara* is derived from the Sanskrit *mri:* death. Mara's sons are caprice, gaiety, and wantonness; his three daughters are delight, discontent, and thirst. The names of the daughters in Sanskrit are Rati, Arati, and Trsna. *Rati* means "sensuous delight," particularly sexual delight. *Arati* therefore means "frigidity" and "coldness." *Trsna* is "thirst," the insatiable thirst, the craving that goes on even after all that we crave for has dropped away and there is left but the rasping that slaking merely aggravates.

Those who have sat in *sesshin* or serious practice are familiar with Mara. The nameless fears; the hollowness where things become insubstantial; the capricious puns and jokes offered by an unemployed intellect; the laughing and crying; the belligerent frustration; the dry aridity; the sexual imagery; the wanting no matter what, just wanting; the lack of seriousness. . . .

No matter what the time, it is always night when facing Mara. In the earlier legends it was not the sons and daughters of Mara that tempted Buddha but Breugel-like armies equipped with all manner of weapons. The untiring persistence of Mara as he churns out snare after block after barrier after byway after inconsequence is like an army, a demonic army striving to break down the imperturbability of the mind-at-one. At this point even to glance at the passing parade is enough to send Mara cackling and dancing off with the mind shattered into a thousand pieces, the rock dissolved into sand, the mountain a crawling anthill.

At dawn he looked up at the morning star; suddenly he became fully awakened and cried, "Wonder of wonders, all beings are endowed with Buddha-nature."

For the Zen Buddhist this is the heart of the story of Buddha's life. This is the great miracle—the coming to oneself, remembering oneself. It is the completed circle. The awakening of one person is the awakening of the whole universe; if one person can awaken, anyone and anything that has sentience can awaken. But to awaken without guidance, inspiration, or encouragement, to awaken fully because of the inner need that cannot be satisfied with anything less than full awakening, is very remarkable.

Zen Buddhists venerate Shakyamuni Buddha because he was a remarkable man, and through his great exertions and unflinching resolve, he reopened a way and taught that way to all who would listen. Central to that way is awakening and the integration of awakening into daily life. The veneration of Shakyamuni therefore also means opening ourselves to the great possibility of awakening. To read the story simply as the account of a great man is to miss the essence; to read it just as an affirmation of awakening is to miss the fact.

—·—·—·—·—·—·—·—·—·—·—·—·—·—·—

Someone asked Buddha,
Are you a god?
No, I am not a god.
Are you a deva?
No, I am not a deva.
Are you a human being?
No, I am not a human being.
Then what are you?
I am awakened.

—·—·—·—·—·—·—·—·—·—·—·—·—·—·—

CHAPTER TWO

Gleanings

THE FOUR NOBLE TRUTHS

Suffering
Birth is suffering; old age is suffering; sickness is suffering; death is suffering; likewise sorrow, grief and lamentation, and despair are suffering. To be together with things we do not like is suffering; to be separated from things we like is suffering. Not to get what we want, that also is suffering. In a word, this body, this fivefold mass based upon grasping, is suffering.

The Cause of Suffering
It is that craving which gives rise to fresh rebirth and, bound by greed for pleasure, now here, now there, finds ever fresh delight. It is the sensual craving, the craving for individual existence, the craving to have done with individual existence.

The End of Suffering
It is the utter passionless cessation of, the giving up, the forsaking, the release from, the absence of longing for, this craving.

The Noble Path
It is right views, right aim, right speech, right action, right living, right effort, right mindfulness, right contemplation.

PRACTICE

Wake Up
Vigilance is the path to life eternal, and thoughtlessness the

path to death. The vigilant do not die; the thoughtless are as dead already.

Be Present

Whether going out or returning, the *bhikkhu* acts with full awareness; whether looking ahead or looking around, he acts with full awareness; whether bending his arm or straightening it, he acts with full awareness; in taking his overrobe, bowl, and spare underrobe, he acts with full awareness; whether eating or drinking, he acts with full awareness; whether walking, standing, or sitting, whether resting or awake, whether talking or silent, he acts with full awareness.

Follow the Breath

A monk goes to the forest or to the root of a tree or to an empty place and sits down with his legs crossed, keeping his body erect and his mind alert. Ever mindful, he breathes in; mindful, he breathes out. Breathing in long, he knows, I breathe in long; breathing out long, he knows, I breathe out long. Breathing in short, he knows, I breathe in short; breathing out short, he knows, I breath out short. "Experiencing the whole breath body, I shall breathe." In thus he trains himself.

GOAL

The End of Suffering

For the attached there is wandering, but for the unattached there is no wandering; without wandering there is serenity; when there is serenity, there is no craving; without craving there is neither coming nor going; without coming or going there is neither passing away nor being reborn; without passing away or being reborn there is neither this life nor the next, nor anything between them. It is the end of suffering.

The Heart's Release

The essentials of the holy life do not consist in the profits of gain, honor, and good name; nor yet in the profits of observing moral rules; nor yet in the profits of knowledge and insight; but the sure hearts release, brethren—that, brethren, is the meaning, that is the essence, that is the goal of living the holy life.

Awakening

Beyond Thought
There is that sphere wherein is neither earth nor water, fire nor air; it is not the infinity of space, nor the infinity of perception; it is not nothingness, nor is it either idea or nonidea; it is neither this world nor the next, nor is it both; it is neither the sun nor the moon.

It neither comes nor goes; it neither abides nor passes away; it is not caused, established, begun, supported; it is the end of suffering.

The Unborn
There is an unborn, unbecome, unmade, unconditioned. If there were not an unborn, unbecome, unmade, unconditioned, then we could not here know any escape from the born, become, made, conditioned.

But since there is an unborn, unbecome, unmade, unconditioned, then we know there is an escape from the born, become, made, conditioned.

Beyond All Form
My doctrine implies thinking of what is beyond thought, performing what is beyond performance, speaking of what is beyond words, and practicing what is beyond practice.

The Way

The Teacher Shows the Way
Here we have nirvana, here we have the way to nirvana, and here stand I as instructor of the Way. Yet some of my disciples, thus advised and trained by me, do attain nirvana, and others do not attain.

What do I in the matter? The Tathagata is the one who shows the Way.

Test of Truth

Now, Kalamas, do not ye go by hearsay nor by what is handed down by others nor by what people say nor by what is stated on the authority of your traditional teachings. Do not go by reasoning nor by inferring nor by argument as to method nor from reflection on and the approval of an opinion nor out of respect thinking a recluse must be deferred to. But, Kalamas, when you know of yourselves that these teachings are not good, that they are blameworthy, that they are condemned by the wise, that these teachings when followed out and put in practice conduce to loss and suffering—then reject them.

Be an Island unto Oneself

And whoever, Ananda, now or after I am dead, shall be an island unto themselves and a refuge to themselves shall take to themselves no other refuge. But those seeing truth as an island, seeing truth as a refuge shall not seek refuge in anyone but themselves. It is these, Ananda, among my disciples who shall reach the Further Shore. But they must make the effort themselves.

Not to Trust One's Own Intelligence

Be careful not to depend on your own intelligence; it is not to be trusted. Take care not to come in contact with physical attraction; such contacts result in calamity. Only when you have reached the stage of *arhat* can you depend on your own intelligence.

The Trappist's Dilemma[1]

The Trappist order used to have a rule of absolute silence in the monasteries. Monks could communicate only by signs, and even these were not to be used except in exceptional cases. A Trappist father tells the following story:

A confusing situation cropped up in choir and went on for quite some time. The brother next to a priest kept prostrating himself, and this began to bother the priest. Prostrating was called "knuckling," and one would knuckle to express humility or to ask God's forgiveness for some imperfection or sin. It was called knuckling because one would prostrate on all fours with the knuckles of one's hand on the floor and his head by his knees.

This brother kept knuckling, and the priest in question began to think that these prostrations occurred because of something he, the priest, was doing—or that something about him was bothering the brother who was knuckling. They would be singing or chanting, and all of a sudden the brother would knuckle. The priest wondered whether there was something wrong with him: Was he singing out of key? Or perhaps he had body odor, or the smell of his breath was bad.

The priest became more and more certain that he was the cause of the brother's knuckling all the time, because he felt that he must be doing something the brother resented—a resentment the brother then felt guilty about.

This doubt gnawed away at the priest for a long time, at least six months. This seemed even a lot longer than it was because in those days the monks spent whole days in the choir, and he had no one to whom he could talk about the problem.

Finally he made up his mind that he had had enough and was determined to get to the bottom of the whole affair. So he decided to speak to the father superior about the matter. He did so and asked the father superior to find out what he was doing that so disturbed the brother.

In a few days the father superior called him into the office with the answer. He told the priest, "He does not know that you exist."

—·—·—·—·—·—·—·—·—·—·—·—·—·—

When the wooden man sings his song,
the stone maiden moves to dance.

—·—·—·—·—·—·—·—·—·—·—·—·—·—

Shrinking Zen

Back in the late sixties, a member of the Rochester Zen Center asked Eric Fromm, "Is Zen of any value as a psychotherapy?" Fromm is said to have replied, "Zen is the *only* psychotherapy!" If one reads his paper *Zen Buddhism and Psychoanalysis*,[1] one is led to believe that Fromm would also say, "Zen is only a psychotherapy." What is the relationship between these two, Zen and psychotherapy, to each other and to us as human beings? Are some of the better psychotherapies Zen in a three-piece suit? Or alternatively, does the practice of Zen make psychotherapy redundant? Fromm, quoting D. T. Suzuki, says:

> It is the object of Zen, therefore, to save us from going crazy or being crippled. This is what I mean by freedom, giving true play to all our creative and benevolent impulses inherently lying in our hearts. Generally we are blind to this fact that we are in possession of all the necessary faculties that will make us happy and loving towards one another.

Fromm goes on to say:

> This description of Zen's aim could be applied without change as a description of what psychoanalysis aspires to achieve: insight into one's own nature, the achievement of freedom, happiness and love, liberation of energy, salvation from being insane or crippled. [2]

It is a seductive thought.

When Zen was introduced into the Western world, it was naturally viewed within the framework and perspective of what was already known—three fundamental frames of reference offered themselves: philosophy, religion, and psychotherapy. Considerable work has been done to show the relationship between Zen and the work of Wittgenstein, Heidegger, and Whitehead,[3] to name but three philosophers; and in the field of religion, the works of St. John of the Cross, Meister Eckehart, St. Benedict, and the anonymous author of *The Cloud of Unknowing* have all been compared to Zen teaching. The same kind of thing happened when Buddhism first appeared in China. There it had to make its peace with Confucianism and Taoism. Indeed, the limitations imposed upon our thinking by our adherence to labels become apparent when we realize that what we know as Zen Buddhism is not simply the outcome of Buddhism alone but is an amalgam of many strands of wisdom and understanding. When one sees into the "truth," it is form-less reality. But to convey some of its flavor to others, words, concepts, and ideas become necessary; and those that are near-est at hand, and that others already have some grasp of, are used. In this way there is some semblance of communication. But picking up words, concepts, and ideas involves carrying over *expectations* as well as meanings. These expectations (or attitudes and mind-sets) are, in turn, filters with which we edit experience.

Zen has fallen on hard times in the West; scarcely a Zen center exists that doesn't have its own brand of malaise. Superficially, we could point a finger at the leaders; many have apparently let down the side through drink, sexuality, power plays, intransigence. But closer inspection soon dispels the illu-sion that we know whom to blame, by showing that this defec-tion is itself a symptom of some greater concern: How does an Eastern-style spirituality, nurtured primarily in the fifteen hun-dred years after the birth of Buddha in India, China, and Korea, fit in with the Western world? Failure to address this question seriously may well be the cause of much of the turmoil and confusion surrounding the practice. What affronts us is not a fact but the violation of expectations. For example, if we do not get an increase in pay at the end of a month, we are not upset *unless we had expected one.* Regularly the check comes at the end of the month, and regularly it is put in the bank without question or comment. If, however, at the beginning of the month someone told us that we were gettting a raise, whether we feel we deserve one or not, we'll get upset and frustrated if the raise is not reflected on the check.

If Zen is a religion or psychotherapy, then what we in the West expect of religion or psychotherapy we shall expect of Zen (and probably much more). If these expectations are not met, then either Zen has failed, we have failed, or those teaching Zen have failed. If an awakened man is a kind of saint and this particular awakened man does not behave as a saint, then there's something wrong with him or with Zen. That Zen is supposed to help us get rid of our expectations does not help, because this itself is an expectation embedded in our psychotherapeutic view that we can make conscious the unconscious. *Where there is id, let there be ego.* This, as Fromm points out, means that we transcend the filters of language, logic, and taboos that express expectations.

Seeing Zen as the *only* psychotherapy, seeing it as the means whereby, in Suzuki's terms, we are able to give "true play to all our creative and benevolent impulses [and discover] that we are in possession of all the necessary faculties that will make us happy and loving towards one another," has its counterpart in the view that Zen is *only* a psychotherapy. This is a belief that many teachers have consciously or unconsciously taught in one way or another and that too many students have accepted. At one time Zen was thought to be the cure-all, and with that belief came the expectation that anyone who kept his or her legs crossed for more than an hour should be free of all ailments, physical and psychological. How many people have sat in meditation fully expecting it to be the solution to all life's problems? This mistaken point of view was also reinforced by teachers who pointed out the "faults" of students, with the implication that Zen would in some way be instrumental in eradicating the fault and with the further implication that if it did not, then the student was not sufficiently "spiritually advanced." The judgment of "senior" students by "junior" students was endemic. Even the confession and repentance ceremony was marred by this expectation. Instead of being an opportunity for true reflection and remorse, it became a way by which people constantly promised themselves, and others, a brighter and better future with "shortcomings" and "faults" eradicated, not taking into account that these shortcomings were more often than not the shadow of what was best and brightest in them and that the eradication of the one would mean the elimination of the other. Personality idiosyncrasies and temperamental differences were confused with faults, and these same faults were confused with klesà, or defilements. But klesà arise from a basic split in the wholeness of a person due to his or her having assumed a human body and are therefore common, in various forms, to us all.

Modern psychotherapy has come into being as the counterpoint to the modern psyche. The picture that Freud drew of the client's ego absorbing or reclaiming the unconscious (much as the Dutch reclaimed the land from the Zuider Zee with a system of dykes and dams) says much about not only the aims of the psychoanalyst but also the aims of the modern psyche: the opposition of the "reality" principle to the "pleasure" principle, the integration of God into the psyche, the taming of the instincts within a reasoned enclosure—all of which moreover tended to support the ongoing illusion of an autonomous and distinct agent in control—was not simply Freud's creation, it was also his discovery. What was significant about Freud's work was not so much that it "cured" psychological illness as that it provided a way of talking about what, up till then, had no socially accepted articulation. It was indeed the new mythology couched within the broader and more embracing mythology of Science. The author Martin Gross says:

> When educated man lost faith in formal religion, he required a
> substitute belief that would be as reputable in the last half of the
> twentieth century as Christianity was in the first. Psychology
> and psychiatry have now assumed the special role. They offer
> mass belief, a promise of a better future, opportunity for confes-
> sion, unseen mystical workings and a trained priesthood of
> helping professionals devoted to servicing the paying-by-the-
> hour communicants.[4]

He adds: "Today psychology is an art, science, therapy, religion, moral code, lifestyle, philosophy and cult."[5]

That psychotherapy is a child of the times is underscored by a 1938 study in which it was shown that the ideals of Western psychotherapy share those of Protestantism: "Individualism, self reliance, self sacrifice, enhancement of wealth and social status and rationalism were recurring themes of both."[6] Conversely, the ideals of Japanese Naikan therapy and Morita therapy stress respect for authority, gratitude toward superiors, and responsibility toward subordinates. Nor is there an intense emphasis on "egalitarianism" or "independence." Japanese therapies tend to be less goal-oriented and tend to concede the more powerful and determinative nature of external social and environmental forces.[7]

However, to say that psychotherapy is a replacement or substitute for Christianity may be misleading; it might be truer to say that just as Christianity crystallized out of an earlier cultural "gel," so psychotherapy has crystallized out of the twentieth-century gel, a major element of which is the absorption of the Deity into the psyche. "To ego-centric modern man the prospect of self instead of God seated at the center of a world's philosophical system is exquisitely attractive."[8] A national newspaper's headlines at the time of the discovery of the structure of DNA read, GOD MAY NOW MOVE OVER, and a rather large and popular book on the recent developments of genetic research is called *Eighth Day of Creation.* [9]

Inherent in the modern psyche is another myth, the myth of progress and evolution. Progress is the means by which evolution is attained, and the goal of evolution as currently understood is for humankind (alias the technocrat) to become God by "conquering" or "harnessing" the forces of nature. Psychotherapy is the apotheosis of this drive toward progress in that its ultimate aim is to rescue humanity from this drive toward perfection. It is, thus, the ultimate act of progress. Norman O. Brown says:

> Psychoanalysis offers a theoretical framework for exploring the possibilities of a way out of the nightmare of endless progress

and endless Faustian discontent, a way out of the human neurosis, a way out of history. . . . The grip of the dead hand of the past would be loosened, and man would be ready to live instead of making history, to enjoy instead of paying back old scores and debts and to enter that state of Being which was the goal of his Becoming.[10]

So it is not surprising that there is a plethora of methods, styles, and aims of psychotherapy. One only has to think of the great names—Freud, Jung, Adler, Fromm, Horney, Klein, Frankl, Asseglioni, Reich, Rank, Erikson—to realize what a panoply of prophets appeared in the firmament. Have a marital problem? A problem of impotence, drug abuse, sex abuse, child abuse, wife abuse, too little energy, too much energy, a lack of confidence? Lack love, creativity, personality? Have no fear: some sessions with the therapists will resolve the problem, will release us, in the words borrowed by Fromm from Suzuki, to "all our creative and benevolent impulses inherently lying in our hearts" and show us that "we are in possession of all the necessary faculties that will make us happy and loving towards one another." Normality now (at least, in the Western world) is "fulfilling one's potential," "expressing oneself," "doing one's thing," conquering the depths of the Zuider Zee not only of the unconscious but also of the tedium of existence, by turning it into fun and *achievement*. With Madison Avenue up ahead and psychotherapy behind, nothing is now impossible.

Or is it?

A British psychologist has spent some time researching the claims of psychotherapy, and one of his more interesting and encouraging findings is that "Roughly two-thirds of a group of neurotic patients will recover or improve to a marked extent within about two years of the onset of their illness, whether they are treated by means of psychotherapy or not."[11] This is encouraging for us but not necessarily for psychotherapists, who might be expected to get better results (but which unfortunately does not seem to be the case). Even Jung claimed that only a third of his patients were cured, with another third being helped by his counseling.

Other studies tend to support this (what might be called

from the psychotherapeutic viewpoint) pessimism. A study was conducted on 650 underprivileged boys, ages six to ten, believed to be potential delinquents.

> By a coin toss half were assigned to a treatment group, the other half was untreated. The treated children were turned over to counselors who used either Freudian therapy methods or the client-centered techniques of psychologist Carl Rogers. The experiment lasted eight years, after which time the youngsters were evaluated.

> The statistical result unnerved the faithful. At first look it has all the ingredients of a heartwarming psychological drama. Of 70 "likely" delinquents given preventive psychotherapy, only 23 had committed serious delinquent acts. The counselors reported two-thirds of the boys "substantially benefited."

> The results were impressive until they checked the untreated control group. The unpsychologised, uncounseled boys proved to have fewer delinquent episodes than their treated peers. The treated boys were involved in 264 offenses while the untreated committed only 218 offenses.[12]

Other researchers have backed sugar placebo (Latin for "I shall please") pills against psychotherapy and have not done too badly: "Placebos too often yield improvement figures very close to therapy figures. . . . Between 50 and 76 percent of patients taking only placebos showed improvement, about the same percentage showing positive results for psychotherapy."[13]

Another researcher, Dr. Frank, has put the sugar wafer up against psychotherapy:

> with poor results for the talking cure. Psychiatric patients were interviewed and tested on various measures including a Mean Discomfort Score (MDS). They were given what was called a "new pill not yet on the market." They were also informed that it was known to be nontoxic and was believed to help patients with complaints similar to theirs.

> The patients returned one week, then two weeks later and were

followed up periodically. *The placebo-takers improved more rapidly than the therapy patients.*[14]

Two psychologists, L. D. Goodsten and J. O. Cites, studied thirty-three academically poor students who took summer-session courses. The students were split into three groups: one received psychological counseling, the second was contacted but did not seek counseling, the third was not even contacted. The results were once again professionally disturbing. *The uncontacted group did the best academically.*[15]

It is not my intention to discredit psychotherapy or to try to prove that it is a waste of time. On the contrary, all that is being suggested is that we may have to be somewhat circumspect in determining exactly what the benefits are not only of psychotherapy but also of Zen. The results of therapy may not have fallen into the categories that the test set up, so they therefore remained undetected. These test categories almost certainly would have been derived from our cultural expectations, which, as has been noted, are dominated by the notion of greater control. If the placebo does as well as the talk cure, it may not mean that the talk cure is no good as much as it means that the placebo has more value than we normally credit. Perhaps therapy cannot deal with delinquency, because it has something much more important to attend to in the person being analyzed.

These tests would not necessarily have been news to Freud or, for that matter, to Fromm. At one point Fromm says, "the change of this or that neurotic character is not possible without pursuing the more radical aim of the complete transformation of the person."[16] He comes back to this same point later: "It may well be that the relatively disappointing results of character analysis are due precisely to the fact that the aims for the cure of the neurotic character *were not radical enough.*"[17] Whether this radical transformation of the person is subject to the kind of test that modern psychologists would like to give is an interesting point. One wonders what the Mean Discomfort Test would have revealed in Ramana Maharshi when he sat in the temple basement covered with ants, or in Tolstoy after his conversion, or in St. John of the Cross hunched up in the dungeon of the monastery in which he was imprisoned.

Again, this is not to defend psychotherapy any more than it is to attack it. Rather keep in mind the original questions: Is Zen the *only* psychotherapy, or is it *only* a psychotherapy—or are we comparing apples and grapeshot? Traditionally, psychotherapy, at the very least, was supposed to improve the functioning of an individual and help develop interpersonal relations. Now results from tests indicate that this does not necessarily seem to be happening. Can Zen do better? If it is the *only* psychotherapy, could Zen have something that the therapies do not have, some vital ingredient that is lacking?

As long as we are working within the expectations from a society having the superman (or superwoman) complex, the resurrection of God at the wheel of a BMW eating a Big Mac with fries, Zen will be at best a constant mystery, at worst a disappointment. There is the story of a Chinese emperor who dispatched a messenger to find a renowned Zen master. The messenger searched far and wide and finally came to a village where his questions were no longer received with a blank stare and shake of the head, but with a nod and a smile.

"Yes, I have heard something about a Zen master living around here. I think you'll find him under the bridge with the beggars."

"Under the bridge with the beggars!? How will I recognize him?"

"Oh, that is easy. Take a melon with you; he loves melons."

There are many who think that taking Zen into everyday life means a kind of superattentiveness, never forgetting anything, never missing anything. A beginner once criticized me very seriously because on a walk together I passed a Coke can just outside the gates of the center without picking it up; another told me that on an early visit to a Zen center his heart sank when he saw that the Roshi's legs were obviously very stiff and painful after a round of sitting. What would they say about this Zen master under the bridge with the beggars! Why isn't he out there clearing up the world's problems, compassionately dispensing the treasures that have come down to him from heaven? What kind of Zen master can be recognized only because he likes melons? Where is all that snap, crackle, and pop. he is supposed to have, those piercing hawklike eyes? Where is all the evidence of social adjustment, creativity?

In the *Mumonkan* there is the koan of Joshu's asking Nansen, "What is the Way?" and Nansen's replying, "Everyday mind is the Way." Someone, giving a talk on this koan, said that Nansen obviously meant everyday mind purged of all its conflicts, greed, contradictions, and pain. But did he? If so, then one must recast Joshu's question, "What is the Way (to purify the mind like that)?" It is quite evident that Nansen was referring to everyday mind as we all know it. Even the everyday mind of the neurotic is the Way.

The word *way* means not only the path, but the *way* to walk the path and the *goal* of that walking. Everyday mind is the Way, the way to walk the Way, and the goal of the Way. To say that the goal of Zen is therefore to save us from going crazy or being crippled, to give "true play to all the creative and benevolent impulses inherently lying in our hearts," is misleading. This *may* be a consequence of the practice of Zen, but it cannot be its aim.

Some people feel that because Krishnamurti said something similar to Nansen, or because they can logically understand the meaning of the expression "Everyday mind is the Way," then they understand what this koan is all about. Others feel that because they can imitate the motions of eating rice from a bowl and then washing the dishes, they have "passed" the koan and can go on to the next one. But everyday mind is *it*. It is a bottomless abyss, or as Nansen says: it is like vast space.

To see into this or any other koan is *something* like reading a poem. One reads the poem and says, "Oh, I understand, how great!" Then later he or she reads the poem again and says, "Oh, I thought I had understood the poem—*now* I understand it!" The second time is different from the first, but who knows what that difference is, how it can be measured, or how it can be proved? One says that Beethoven is greater than the Beatles, but wherein lies the difference? If you say that there are some who would not agree, then you simply help me make my point. Is it really, as many would say, but a matter of taste? Or is it a matter of *depth,* something with which our society, in its urge toward measurement, toward proof, with the related urge toward egalitarianism, has lost contact? One can read a good poem a hundred times and still say, "*Now* I understand."

So it is, in a way, with Nansen's everyday mind—not that there is any greater understanding, because "greater understanding" is itself an aspect of everyday mind. (But we have to be careful how many nits we pick out of words.) In Zen it is said, "He [or she] goes into the forest without disturbing a blade of grass; he [or she] enters the pool without creating a ripple." Seeing ever deeper into the truth that everyday life is the Way is the way by which we take our practice into everyday life. But we do this without disturbing things, without the fanfare that Suzuki and Fromm would blow. Zen is not the reason for doing something, nor the reason for not doing it.

In the koan Joshu asks, "But how do we know that we are on the Way?" This is the question that tortures so many Westerners, brought up as we are in the age of pragmatism, the age of "if it works, it is OK; if it does not, then throw it out." Because of this pragmatism, we look to psychotherapy as the Western model for an Eastern way.

The aim of Zen is to *wake up,* but insofar as waking up has no steps or stages, no causes or obstructions, it cannot strictly speaking be called an "aim." Someone said about faith, "If faith, then faith." Likewise we could say, "If waking up, then wake up." It is the ultimate in the simple, but that does not mean it is easy. To "wake up" means that we live in the midst of our own, and the world's, contradictions. It is precisely seeing contradictions as contradictions that keeps us in the stream of birth and death. The very force of birth and death, its vitality and élan, comes from the will to resolve contradiction. The wheel of *samsara* revolves ever around alternative solutions and resolutions, leaving unsolved and unresolved part of the contradictions to nag and worry. Not to resolve contradictions, to live in the midst of them, to see everyday mind as no promise of superman's breaking out of all the cul de sacs and dilemmas, is very painful; it is antilife (and death) and is what was once called purgatory, a purgatory that moreover can go on for years. Joshu said, "Only sit down quietly, say, for twenty or thirty years and if you still fail to understand, you can cut off this old monk's head." To sit down quietly, not to disturb a blade of grass, not to make a ripple. With the psychological expectations of the Westerner reclaiming the Zuider Zee, building dams and canals, how is this sitting quietly to be understood?

Of course, the question inevitably arises, "Should one not then seek psychotherapy?" But that is a question to ask the therapist. Seeking therapy, working through conflicts and dilemmas, is part of everyday life, too, just as complaining and groaning about the pain, about the Way, about the teacher, is everyday mind. If one has a financial problem, one resolves it at a financial level, even if it means pawning one's watch. If one wishes to change oneself, or some aspect of oneself, therapy may help, but a therapist is the best judge. It was expressed very succinctly once in a saying: "Render unto Caesar the things that are Caesar's, and render unto God the things that are God's."

What then is the connection between Zen and psychotherapy? There's an old Indian saying: "Stone, no dog. Dog, no stone." This seems to mean that one day when a dog came barking and snapping at someone, the person looked everywhere for a stone to hurl at the dog but was unable to find one. Then later he found a stone, but by then the dog had given up. But there is another way to understand it. Looking at a stone dog, one can admire how well the artist has captured the likeness, the form, of the dog; in this case, one does not see the stone. Or one can admire the substance, the stone, the wonderful veins that streak through it; in this case, there is no dog. Psychotherapy is concerned with the form and content of mind, Zen with the mind itself. Psychotherapy is directed toward the forms that awareness takes, forms that inevitably end in conflict and struggle; Zen looks to awareness, nonreflected awareness, itself.

> *Form is no other than Emptiness*
> *Emptiness no other than Form*

_._._._._._._._._._._._._._._._._._

> *Zen master Rinzai said,*
> *Followers of the way, mind is without form and pervades the ten directions:*
> *In the eye it is called seeing,*
> *In the ear it is called hearing.*
> *In the nose it smells odors,*
> *In the mouth it holds converse.*
> *In the hands it grasps and seizes,*
> *In the feet it runs and carries.*
> *Fundamentally it is one pure radiance; divided it becomes harmoniously united spheres of sense. Since the mind is nonexistent, wherever you go you are free.*

_._._._._._._._._._._._._._._._._._

CHAPTER FIVE

The Rabbi's Distress

A true story is told about a rabbi whose custom it was to hear one by one the confessions and problems of his disciples. The disciples would go into the rabbi's room for the interview and, afterward, would leave the door ajar, signaling the next in line that the rabbi was free. During one hour a chief disciple noticed that the rabbi's door had been closed for quite a long while, and the waiting room was full of anxious disciples. Finally he could wait no longer and, contrary to custom, gently pushed the door open to see what was going on. He found to his amazement the rabbi sitting with his head buried in his hands. The chief disciple asked what the matter was, and in reply the rabbi simply leaped up and demanded that the community declare a fast for him and that they assemble for afternoon prayers.

When the rabbi seemed more settled, two disciples asked him about what had happened. The rabbi answered that when he listened to people's problems, sins, and worries, he always looked inside himself to find a similar disposition to what his disciple was talking about. The last disciple he listened to told such a terrible story that the rabbi could find nothing in his own life to match it. "I was struck down by this," said the rabbi, "because it could only mean that such a similarity did exist, but I had felt the need to suppress it in myself."

_. _. _. _. _. _. _. _. _. _. _. _. _. _.

*There is no better method of approaching this Word
than in silence, in quiet; we hear it aright in unknowing. To one who knows naught, it is clearly revealed.*

_. _. _. _. _. _. _. _. _. _. _. _. _. _.

PART 2

Buddhism and Christianity

CHAPTER SIX

The Christian and Buddhist Dark Night of the Soul

Dear Friend,

You write to say you wonder why I have suggested that you read *The Dark Night of the Soul* by St. John of the Cross. You ask what the writings of a sixteenth-century Christian monk have to do with the Zen meditation practice of a twentieth-century Canadian. Doesn't he have quite a different set of values? Is there, you ask, no difference between what he calls union with God and what the Zen tradition calls *satori*? He says quite specifically that union can be accomplished only by the grace of God, yet in Zen God is not a consideration. Furthermore, he avows that he is writing not for the general public but for his fellow monks. Monks in sixteenth-century Spain would have been used to privation and discomfort of the kind that we could never tolerate. You say that you are discouraged by reading St. John and wonder whether the feeble efforts that you make are worth anything at all alongside the asceticism demanded by St. John. The life you live in no way approaches the privation of even a modern-day monk.

Monastic and Lay Practice

I can understand these concerns, but even so, some of them are misplaced. One should not be concerned because one's practice is a lay practice, nor should one feel handicapped because one has a family to look after and a job to do.

Some people naturally gravitate toward a monastic life,

but not always for the best reasons. Indeed, the motivation for becoming a monk is different for different people. I remember on one occasion visiting a commune of ex-hippies in New Brunswick. It was a sad experience. In a way, when they left to set up their commune, they were inspired by a kind of monastic calling. They had longed for a cleaner, purer kind of existence, based upon community rather than conflict and competition, simplicity rather than acquisition. But when I met them, they were weary, disappointed, and despairing. In truth, when they dropped out of society, they had had a very naive view of life and of the way to resolve its dilemmas. They had perceived what was wrong with the system and felt that all they had to do was just drop out and set up another, different kind of system, free of the errors and complications of the old one. This naive, idealistic view of the world is at the bottom of some people's flight to a monastery.

Other people go to a monastery because they have a romantic notion about being a "good" person. I wonder how many young women incarcerated themselves in convents with the romantic notion of being the bride of Christ and living in a kind of perpetual spiritual honeymoon? It is an inspired and wonderful dream, but it is only a dream. The sad thing is that one can later so easily identify these young women now grown old, bitter, and disillusioned, all their dreams and hopes crushed by the reality they met. One meets them when traveling on the Metro in Montreal, lost souls who never lived.

Life is complex, in or out of a monastery. We cannot deal with this complexity by closing our eyes to it. All that does is put off the day when we have to come face to face with it, and the longer this day is put off (as the old, bitter nuns were to realize), the greater the debt we incur. One essential realization that comes when we do face up to the situation is that we are not good, and others bad. As Solzyhenitsyn said, "The line between good and evil does not go along the boundaries of different nations, but through the very center of our own heart." All of us are an inextricable mixture of good and bad, kind and cruel, loving and hating. The threads of life are inextricably woven together in one grand tapestry that we call "experience," and the threads are of all colors. Trying to be good alone can have disastrous effects. A story is told in Zen of a governor who had attended a retreat with a famous Zen master, Nansen. After the retreat the two were walking and talking in the garden, and Nansen asked the governor, "How will you govern the people?" The governor replied, "With wisdom and compassion." "Then every last one of them will suffer," exclaimed Nansen.

Another wrong motive is the belief that the world offers distractions and that if only we could run away from these distractions, the work on ourselves would be correspondingly easier. But the source of our problems lies not in the world but in the way we view the world, what we demand of it, and what we refuse to pay so that these demands may be met. It is the viewer that must change, not the view. Our life is the outcome of what we are, and what we are is the outcome of the way we think and of the way we see the world. However many times we change our location, our jobs, our spouses, or other elements of our life, we still carry the same thoughts, the same reactions, and the same way of viewing the world and others.

A story tells of an old man who was sitting by the side of a road that went from one city to another. He asked a traveler, "Where are you coming from?" The traveler pointed over his shoulder and said, "From that city down the road." "What was it like there?" "Terrible," replied the traveler. "The people were unfriendly. I could not find work. It was an ugly place." "Where are you going to?" asked the old man. "Along to that city up ahead," the traveler answered. "Oh, I know it well," said the old man. "What is it like?" asked the traveler. "Terrible," said the old man. "The people are unfriendly, one can never find work, and it is quite an ugly place." The traveler went on his way, disconsolate. Later another traveler came along, and the old man asked him the same question. "Where are you coming from?" The traveler pointed over his shoulder and said, "From that city down the road." "What was it like there?" "A wonderful place. I had so much work, I could not keep up with it. The people were all wonderful, and really it is quite a beautiful city." "Where are you going to?" asked the old man. "Along to that city up ahead." "Oh, I know it well," said the old man. "What is it like?" asked the traveler. "Wonderful," said the old man. "The people are friendly, one can find all the work one wants, and it is quite a beautiful place." The traveler went on his way, rejoicing.

With all the above in mind, it is as well not to have too romantic an idea about monasteries or feel that monks or nuns have the edge on laypeople when it comes to practice. Zen, as you know, is a part of the Mahayana tradition, and within the Zen tradition are two sutras devoted to the lives and teaching of laymen. All the rest of the sutras are attributed to the Buddha. The fact that these two sutras based upon the lay life exist, as well as the fact that many stories are told about lay Zen practitioners, indicates that lay practice was held in high esteem by masters of the past. What is at issue is the sincerity and honesty with which the spiritual life is led, not the time or place in which one happens to be, nor the particular religion that one happens to follow.

As you know, at the Montreal Zen Center we insist that the center of practice be your home. The most important part of the work you do on yourself is done in the family and at your workplace. Your children, spouse, boss, the clerk at the bank—indeed, all the people whom one meets in a day—can be your teacher. A teacher of monks must beat them, humiliate them, drive them to make greater efforts. A teacher of lay students has it easy. All that he or she has to do is to sit back and let life do the hard work.

When you practice meditation and a monk practices meditation, no difference exists between the problems, dilemmas, uncertainties, and anguish faced by you both. This is quite evident during a sesshin. When you meditate, and above all when you give yourself unreservedly to meditation during a sesshin, you pass through the dark night of the soul to some degree or another—and this is when the teachings of St. John become of greatest value. Forget the rest. Forget about his being a Christian and your not, about his being a monk and your being a layperson, about the sixteenth century and the twentieth century.

DIFFICULTY OF PRACTICE

As you go on in practice, certain crises will occur, times when the bottom will seem to have fallen out of existence. These crises occur because of meditation, although often one may want to give them a more mundane cause. But when you meditate truly, you are giving yourself over to a total reevaluation of your whole way of being, to a reevaluation of the basis of even the way you see the world, yourself, and others. This means that much of what you value now may well come to seem tasteless and futile, that things you have sought after will lose their meaning. This happened also when you were a young child growing into adolescence. Then too you had to let go of toys, of your total dependency on and security in your mother, of your likes and dislikes, and so on, all of which reflected your values at that time. This and other occasions of life, which have been called by someone "passages," evoke feelings of insecurity, self-doubt, anxiety, and many other confused and painful feelings. They too are times of dark night.

You complain that your life has become tasteless, that you have a constant feeling of oppression and anxiety affecting even your sleep. You say you seem to be lost and wonder whether your practice has in some way been faulty or whether you have been abandoned. These are symptoms of someone who has entered the dark night. It was for this reason that I suggested St. John to you. In one very powerful passage he points out that when people "get a glimpse of this concrete and perfect life of the spirit—which manifests itself in the complete absence of all sweetness, in aridity, distaste, and in the many trials that are the true spiritual cross—they flee from it as from death."[1]

THE VALUE OF ST. JOHN FOR THOSE WHO PRACTICE ZEN

Let me try to show you why I feel that St. John can be of value to you. First, of course, you must understand I am not going to try to give any scholarly or systematic dissertation upon St. John. I do not know enough about him to do this, and in any case I am concerned only that you should be able to come to terms with what you are, with your own life and its tribulations, its pains and joys. I am not asking you to learn some obscure theology. St. John gets carried away sometimes by his metaphor of the night and forces some of his explanations to make them fit in with his metaphor. This makes him sometimes difficult to follow. He is somewhat repetitious and so boring. For many, even the language he uses is an obstacle. Trained as he was in the theology of the Middle Ages, threatened as he was by the Inquisition, it is not surprising that he should use the idiom of the ardent Catholic of his time. For people of the twentieth century, this idiom can be difficult to accept. Yet, what a pity it would be if what St. John is trying to say were lost as a consequence.

Therefore, let me use my own experience of more than forty years as a wayfarer, both as a student and later as a teacher, but at the same time refer to St. John constantly as a companion on the way so that I have an authority to support me in what I shall try to do, an authority whom time and the devotion of many devout people have shown to be so completely reliable. When I say I shall use my experience, I do not mean only worldly experience, because, as St. John says, no ordinary experience by itself is of much use. Only the one who has himself traveled along this way, he says, "can have inner awareness of it, but even he cannot express it adequately in words."[2]

St. John suffered greatly in the work he did upon himself, and out of this suffering came wisdom and strength. He was also one of those rare people who are able to reflect upon his suffering and make the results of this reflection available to others. In his essence he is very practical and talks from his own experience, which is both deep and learned but also simple because he too wants the monks he addresses to understand the importance of suffering the dark night in order to attain, in this case, union with God. I believe he did this, moreover, not so that they would just be good Christians but so that, as human beings, they could come to terms fully with what it means to be human. This is what is important. Who am I? What must I do? What is truly meaningful and worthwhile in the face of the certainty of death? How can I cope with the suffering that life unleashes upon me and upon those whom I love? Facing these and similar questions is what I mean by coming to terms fully with what it means to be human.

AWAKENING AND UNION WITH GOD

As you know, my teaching is all about awakening beyond all form, how to come to awakening. Without doing this, without coming to awakening, we are, as a Zen master says, like ghosts clinging to weeds. We may present a most imposing figure dressed in one kind of robe or another; we may be able to expound upon all kinds of scriptures, Buddhist or Christian; we may have endured all kinds of austerities, visited all kinds of masters, be accomplished in all kinds of ways. But even so, we are but camouflaged holes. To come to awakening is the most profound, the most worthwhile, of all human endeavors. By awakening I do not simply mean *kensho,* that moment of awakening for the first time; I mean the integration of it fully into life as we are living it here and now.

But as you also know, my teaching emphasizes knowing yourself as "someone in the world," to know yourself as a good/bad person, a wise man/fool. I often use the metaphor of a landscape: it has hills and valleys, fields and marshes, weeds and flowers; and one accepts it all, takes it all in and says, "This is my home." In the same way we are a bundle of contradictions, of clashing opposites, of failed promises and dashed hopes. Loving and hating, doing good and not doing good, being courageous and being cowardly, we must be able to accept it all, take it all in and say, "This is me." Awakening and getting to know yourself in this way are not two different paths leading in two different directions. Awakening is the path; getting to know yourself to the point of transcending the self is the way to walk the path. As a Zen master once said, "Every day mind is the way."

Because awakening is the fulfillment of our humanity, it means that the spiritual quest is not an endeavor that only specially endowed people can attain to. On the contrary, people who are considered spiritual by the world are so often bound up so tightly in their own convictions and beliefs that they are like flies trapped in a web. All and each of us has the innate potential to awaken; each of us indeed from the very beginning is whole and complete and lacks nothing needed to realize this. But this does not mean that the way is easy and without great difficulties, nor that it does not require great energy and determination to pass through. It is these difficulties in their many guises that plunge us into the dark night of the soul; and without having passed through this, you cannot truly come into your own birthright. It is therefore of this trial that you must undergo to awaken that I shall speak.

SCARCITY OF AUTHENTIC TEACHERS

Unfortunately, the masters of old in the Zen tradition have not left very much in the way of descriptions of this dark night. On the contrary, the many mondo or dialogues between master and disciple, during which it often happens that the disciple comes to awakening, tend to leave us with the impression that it is all so easy, that it is a question of a knack or trick—some secret understanding or skill of the master that is involved. We do not take into account what led up to the encounter, what made the monk ask his question, what deserts he had passed through, what anguish he had known. This is why the work of St. John is so valuable.

In the Christian tradition one speaks of union with God. Whether union with God is the same as, superior to, or inferior to awakening, I will leave to others to judge. The treatise of St. John of the Cross, however, was a source of unfailing inspiration to me during my own years of travail, and I have often recommended him to others in the hope that he will provide them too with some sustenance to support them in their way.

In the very beginning of his work, St. John says that he is writing both for the beginner and for the more advanced, not only to help them free themselves of all that is temporal but also to help them so that they are not weighed down by the spiritual. What is required is to be completely free and naked. These are the basic requirements for union with God. Similarly, when practicing Zen meditation you must divest yourself of all belief that you are *something,* however refined that something may be, and you must free yourself also from all that you know, including all that you know about Zen and Buddhism, in order that knowing itself can escape from the multitude of sheaths and coverings by which it is buried, and can shine through by its own luminescence.

Unfortunately, the number of teachers of Zen Buddhism in the West is very small, and of these only a few have themselves come to awakening and then passed through the refining fire required after the initial breakthrough. One of the sad things that has arisen because of this is a skepticism that has entered into the Zen practice of many people about the value of awakening, as well as about the possibility of Westerners being able to attain to it. The doubts about awakening are raised by those who themselves have not awakened. This same problem existed in St. John's day, and he too laments that many people who have the necessary disposition for spiritual work remain in an elementary stage of communion with God, either because they lack the determination or understanding or because no one is available to lead them on the right path. Although it is true that we are all whole and complete and although it is true this wholeness is constantly wanting to shine through, these truths can nevertheless be obstructed by faulty understanding or by incorrect practice.

St. John points out that many spiritual teachers, because they themselves have no experience of their own to draw upon, are prone to hinder and harm those whom they presume to lead. Often, for example, someone on the way encounters darkness and dryness and is likely to believe that he is completely lost. Such a person, "being filled with darkness, misery, afflictions, and temptations will perhaps meet someone who speaks like Job's comforters, telling him or her that he or she is suffering from melancholy or depression or from a morbid frame of mind." This is no less true in our own day. We too have our own Job's comforters. Often these "counselors" advise the person to stop, to turn back, since the practice is bringing nothing but increased pain and anguish. But giving such advice simply increases the trials. "For it may well be that the greatest affliction that the person feels is the knowledge of his or her own misery."

Often these "counselors" try to interpret this state in a psychological way and encourage the person to try to find some particular traumas or some person in the past who can be blamed. St. John says these counselors make their victims "examine and reexamine their past lives, demanding they make general confession." It is vital that a distinction be made between suffering that is induced as a consequence of spiritual work and suffering that arises because of psychological maladjustment. Confusing the two can only add immeasurably to the suffering of the person. The dark night of the soul can easily be confused with depression, and sometimes medication is even prescribed that can only throw the hapless victim into greater torment still. However, it is only one who has passed through the dark night who has the authority to help another through. Otherwise, it is like one who, not being able to swim himself, nevertheless exhorts another to plunge into the foaming waves. Moreover, it is only one who has experienced the darkness for himself or herself who truly recognizes the symptoms.

CONFESSION AND DOKUSAN

Confession is an important part of the Christian practice in the same way that *dokusan,* or private encounter with the teacher, is an important part of the practice of Zen Buddhism. Although these two are by no means the same, they have a great deal in common. Both are private and confidential. What a student says to a teacher in dokusan cannot be repeated outside, and naturally this is also true of the confessional. Both require that the student be as honest as the circumstances allow. Although both the confessor and the teacher need to be good psychologists—indeed, it is preferable that the teacher have had some training and practical experience in psychology—nevertheless the primary aim of both the confessional and dokusan is to further the student along the spiritual path, not to play the role of psychological counselor. While it is vital that a spiritual malaise should not be dealt with as though it were a psychological one, so a problem of a psychological nature should be dealt with as such and not simply as though it were a spiritual problem. In some Zen circles it is still believed that zazen is a panacea and will ultimately solve all problems. This is a mistake and can cause a great deal of unnecessary suffering on the part of the practitioner.

Both the confessional and dokusan therefore concern the deepest part of the student, who must have sufficient faith in the teacher or confessor so he or she can be open and honest, willing to reveal and discuss his or her deepest feelings and difficulties. Pride often prevents us from being frank, and this can reach a point where some are too embarrassed to confess their sins or explore their difficulties openly because they are afraid the teacher will think less of them as a consequence.

ON THE HAZARDS OF THE TEACHER-STUDENT RELATIONSHIP

St. John says that pride also causes people to want to be favorites of the teacher and to become intimate with him or her; as a result, they are always envious of and restless about others. One often meets with this same kind of situation in dokusan. This need to be intimate with the teacher is one of the more delicate aspects of the whole teacher-student relationship, particularly when the teacher is of one sex and the student of the other and when neither has taken a vow of chastity. One of the outcomes of spiritual practice is awakening to higher feelings of love and gratitude. Love and gratitude are both expression of unity and are harbingers of awakening and union with God. The opportunity to love another fearlessly with the assurance of complete security, while at the same time feeling that one is loved unconditionally, is rare and precious. However, the erotic often enters into the relationship to some degree or another, not only on the part of the student but on the part of the teacher. The erotic element comes from the personality, from being a "man" in front of a "woman." Love, which comes with the dawn of awakening, is beyond the personality, beyond the opposites of "me" and "you," beyond "man" and "woman," beyond "subject" and "object." One could say one's true nature is love, just as it is true to say one's true nature is whole, One. The erotic in its own sphere is both natural and wonderful, but mixed unwittingly with "spiritual" love, it can create havoc.

Because spiritual love has no subject, no one is affirmed by the love and so no one loses either. Spiritual love cannot be transformed into hatred. The opposite of spiritual love is the dark night of the soul. On the other hand, erotic love comes from the play of two *subjects,* each surrendering voluntarily to be an object for the other. It is essentially concerned with giving and taking the initiative. Each beckons and turns away in such a manner that each affirms the other until each becomes the other. Thus, erotic love, no less than spiritual love, has unity as its basis. In some Tantric systems the erotic and the spiritual are consciously undifferentiated, and one sees this same tendency also with St. John in some of his poetry. For someone who can truly sustain the tension involved in the erotic relationship and who has the capacity for unconditional love, this can be an effective way of helping another. The requirement is that the teacher must constantly sacrifice the affirmation that the relationship offers.

This can, at times, be like walking a tightrope because not only does it require complete honesty on the part of the teacher but it is also essential that the teacher not manipulate his own feelings or his student's feelings according to some preestablished code of conduct. Doing so creates a phony relationship that is soon detected by the student, who then receives mixed signals: the words and conduct say one thing, while the emotional aura and body language say another. This creates feelings not only of mistrust but also of deep betrayal.

Neither should a teacher try to repress his own feelings or the feelings of his student. Love, as we said, often has at first some erotic overtones. To try to repress or deny these brings a false element of reserve into the relationship, which is only effective in the absence of this kind of maneuvering. A Zen story, used as a koan in the later stages of practice, bears upon this problem. An old woman, who lived in China, had given support to a monk for many years. She had a small hermitage built for him and gave him food while he meditated. One day she wondered to what kind of depth his meditation had taken him. Intrigued by the question, she got the help of a young and very beautiful woman. "Please go and embrace him," she instructed the woman, "and then ask him, 'What about it?'"

The young woman visited the monk and straightaway began to embrace and caress him. Then she asked him, "What about it?" "An old tree grows on a cold and hard rock in winter," replied the monk. "Nowhere is there any warmth." The young woman returned and told the old woman what had happened.

"To think that I have looked after that guy for so long!" shouted the old woman in anger. "He showed no compassion for you at all; all he thought about was himself. He did nothing to help you at all. While he did not have to become passionate, he should nevertheless have had some compassion."

She went straightaway to the monk's hut and burned it down.

However, the worst thing a teacher can do is to succumb to the eroticism and have intercourse with his student or even declare his feelings for the student. The possibility of allowing the student to distill out of the situation pure, spiritual love is irrevocably destroyed. The relationship soon becomes just an erotic one and very likely will degenerate into a purely sexual affair in which unity is simply physical junction. Erotic love, as the poetry, songs, and dramas of all the world affirm over and over again, can in a moment turn to violent hatred, causing the teacher and the student to fly apart. Both will feel deeply hurt and humiliated by the other and will react destructively toward the other in one way or another. This can well create deep discord in the community that will grow worse as other students hear of the infidelity of the teacher. This in turn creates jealousy and anger and further feelings of betrayal.

Not only this, but anyone—man or woman—who goes into dokusan with that teacher after it has become known what has been happening finds another "presence" in the relationship.

A sense of a "hidden agenda" of the teacher having more than the student's well-being at heart pervades the dokusan room, and this inhibits the frankness and openness that is essential.

St. John's Book Is Not for All

St. John says that his book is not meant for all and sundry but for certain members of the Order of Mount Carmel. In a similar way, what I am offering is meant in particular for you and people like you who are following an authentic spiritual path. You are following the Rinzai tradition, the tradition that insists upon the practitioner gaining a direct knowing for themselves into the truth that fundamentally we are all whole and complete. You attend sesshin or retreats, and as I said just now, it is during a retreat, particularly a retreat of seven days, that you really appreciate most what St. John is talking about. This is not to say that it is only during this time of retreat that his counsel is applicable. But it will likely be those retreats, or else some sudden reversal of fortune, that precipitates entry into the dark night of the soul.

The Obstacles to Practice

St. John draws a distinction between beginners and those more advanced on the path, whom he calls "progressives." Beginners, he says, advance along the path by meditation, the progressives by contemplation. He points out that because beginners may not have been prepared by the practice of earnestly striving in the virtues, they often have many faults and imperfections. These faults and imperfections are obstacles that prevent beginners from being able to see into the true nature of the situation; therefore, they are inclined to practice for the benefits, "for the consolations and pleasures that they find in the practice." St. John then discusses these imperfections in order that we can understand the real value of passing through the dark night, since it is just this passage that cleanses the soul from all the imperfections he refers to.

One of the great difficulties that many have with the practice of Zen comes from this same tendency to practice for what they can get out of it. Indeed, many are quite stunned when it is suggested that the practice should be done without this commercial attitude. Led to believe by various means in the beauty and peace that come from the practice, the strength and wisdom that emerge from it, many practice trying to grasp the beauty and peace, to seize the strength and wisdom. This tendency is encouraged by many would-be teachers of meditation who either maliciously or unwittingly encourage people in this commercial attitude of giving something to get something, some time in meditation for a period of peace and quiet.

Because this bartering kind of practice is quite opposed to the spirit of true practice, those who practice in this way soon get to the point where they complain about nothing happening. What they mean by this is what they expect—indeed, demand—to happen is not happening. Something, however, is indeed happening; this something is the onset of the dark night. This they resist with all their might, complaining about the poor teaching or about the complicated practice they have been called upon to do, by finding fault with the teacher, and so on. As we shall see, all these things are discussed by St. John under seven headings that are the seven capital sins.

PRIDE

The first barrier to union that St. John deals with is pride. Not only is it a barrier that blocks all of us in some form or another, pride is the most difficult of all sins to overcome and the most persistent. Even after deep kensho it can still be a problem, which is made obvious, for example, by the writings of Hakuin. He had struggled heroically over a long period of time and finally penetrated through to the truth. He said, "It was as if a sheet of ice had been smashed or a jade tower had fallen with a crash." All his former doubts vanished as though ice had melted away. Then he said, "My pride soared up like a majestic mountain, my arrogance surged forward like the tide."[3]

However, our pride is not always so blatant and obvious. St. John points out that it can often be a kind of secret pride that rises in the heart of a person, and because of this they are satisfied with themselves and with their practice. This kind of pride is more or less insuperable because most often it prevents people from even being part of a group, let alone visiting a teacher. St. John says, "They feel compelled to talk to others about spiritual things all the time and even to spend their time teaching others rather than learning themselves," but they rarely have the courage to ask a teacher a real question or expose themselves in any way. On the few occasions they do so, they do not listen to the reply, but, while it is being given, look out of the corner of their eye awaiting the opportunity to make some objection or to ridicule in some way the reply or to give some other sign of their dissatisfaction and contempt.

St. John points out that some students are so eager to be praised and esteemed in all they do that if their teacher does not approve of what they are doing, they consider him or her to be deficient, lacking either in understanding or in spirituality. So they immediately look around for someone else who will fit in with their tastes. They want to be only with people who praise and esteem them, and they flee, as from death, from those who try to correct them and lead them into a safe road, even harboring ill will against them. This kind of person is full of resolutions about what he or she will accomplish but in fact does very little that is worthwhile. It would be of far more value, says St. John, if such a person felt that the teacher and others consider them of no account.

He says sometimes pride can also cause people to work harder than everyone around them and feel that they are the only ones who are really virtuous. In order to convince others about how spiritual they are, they put on an act, practice diligently when they feel they are being watched, and do all kinds of things to be noticed. They take every opportunity to slander others, "beholding," as St. John says, "the mote in their brother's eye while ignoring the beam in their own, straining at another's gnat while swallowing a camel themselves." They often despise others, criticizing their practice because it is not in conformity with their own ideas of how one should do it, and so resemble the Pharisee who boasted of himself, praising God for his own good works and despising the publican.[4]

Pride may make some people look upon their faults paradoxically as of no consequence on one hand, yet on the other they become quite disconsolate upon realizing that they are indeed inflicted with faults and difficulties, because they had believed themselves already to have risen above the level of such problems. Thus, they often become very impatient, even angry, with themselves for their imperfections. Because they are in so much of a hurry to get where they are not, they never really know where they are. They have no firm ground to stand upon, no real contact with themselves, and so their practice is a kind of dream within a dream.

ANGER

St. John says that the second major fault that often accompanies our practice is anger and rage. This rage can be directed by some people at the practice itself and at anyone associated with it. Because they practice in order to gain some pleasant feelings or experiences, many become embittered when their delight in spiritual things comes to an end, and bear that lack of sweetness they have to suffer with a bad grace affecting all that they do. They become irritated at the smallest thing, to the point that no one can tolerate them. Another target for this irritability is the shortcomings of others; they keep watch on those others with a sort of uneasy zeal, sometimes feeling obliged to correct others angrily and to set themselves up as masters of zeal.

If this anger is not directed at others, it can often be directed at themselves when they see their own imperfections. They often become impatient with themselves, so much so that they would be "saints in a day." They often make grand resolutions of what they intend to accomplish, yet as they have little humility and have no misgivings about themselves, the more resolutions they make, the greater their fall and the greater their annoyance because, in St. John's words, "they have to have the patience to wait for what God will give them when it pleases Him." A Zen master said, "I do nothing all day, but leave nothing undone." This is work done in all humility, allowing each moment to reveal its need, and is quite the opposite of work done out of force and effort using the energy of desire and aggression as the motivating power.

SPIRITUAL GLUTTONY

Another problem is spiritual gluttony, which is a fault that many beginners suffer from. Often in the early stages of practice, one is visited by a certain kind of sweetness. People can become very attached to this feeling and so not seek after spiritual purity and discretion. Consequently, they often go to extremes, passing beyond the limits of moderation by which the virtues are acquired and wherein they have their being. Some people, attracted by the pleasures they find therein, punish themselves with penances, while others weaken themselves with fasts greater than their frailty can bear. These people are most imperfect and unreasonable because they set bodily penance before subjection to reason and discretion, which is a sacrifice more acceptable and pleasing to God. As St. John says, "All extremes are vicious, and in behaving thus, persons are working their own will; they grow in vice rather than in virtue because they are acquiring spiritual gluttony and pride in working in this way."

Penance increases the feeling of being in control, of being the one who does things. This feeling of being in control is so pleasant, but at the same time, it is precisely this feeling that is the major block and that has to be surrendered in practice.

In order to remain with the feeling of being in control, these people change or vary or add to what is given to them as a practice. Any obedience on this is so bitter to them indeed that some give up practice altogether because they are given one practice rather than another, while their only pleasure and desire is to do what they themselves are inclined to do. St. John goes on to say, "These people are very insistent that the teacher grant them what they desire, extracting it from him almost by force; and if they are refused, they become as peevish as small children."

ENVY

Another problem more frequently encountered than many would believe is spiritual envy. In St. John's words, "Many people are wont to experience moments of displeasure at the spiritual good of others, which causes them sensible grief at being outstripped on this road, so that they would prefer not to hear others praised and they become displeased at others' virtues and sometimes they cannot refrain from contradicting what is said in praise of others, deprecating it as far as they can. Their annoyance thereat grows because the same is not said of them, for they would fain be preferred in everything."

In a book on koan practice[5] I told of how during my early days as teacher at the Montreal Zen Center, I would spend a good deal of my time counseling members about envy. At the Rochester Zen Center, which at that time was the center the members would visit to attend long retreats, it was the custom to award *raksus* to people who had passed the first koan. A raksu is a square cloth made of strips that is hung around the neck. When a new recipient of a raksu emerged sitting in the *zendo,* it would cause a wave of tension and suffering among those who had not yet been awarded one. The tension came from the struggle to control fierce envy.

Ramana Maharshi tells of a hermit who, so envious was he of Maharshi's state, would roll huge boulders down upon him in an endeavor to inflict some injury upon him. Buddha's cousin, Devadatta, was so envious of Buddha that he made three attempts upon Buddha's life. The third Zen patriarch was poisoned by an envious Taoist. In the koan collection called the Mumonkan, a koan tells of Hui-neng, who became the sixth Patriarch by his teacher, even though he was illiterate, very young, and but a novice. He was pursued by a monk from the same monastery in which Hui-neng had received the transmission, represented by a robe and a bowl, that had been passed on to him by the fifth patriarch. The monk was incensed by the idea that someone such as Hui-neng should be so honored, and he was determined to tear the robe and bowl away from him. It is worth noting that Hui-neng did away with the tradition of passing on the robe and bowl.

Possibly the most telling example of the danger that can be caused by envy is given in the New Testament. Judas, a disciple and friend of Jesus, out of envy betrayed him with a kiss, and so torn was Judas by remorse that he later hanged himself from a tree.

All of this pride, anger, spiritual greed, and envy comes from the basic need each of us has to be the One, to be unique, to be the center. I have written about this at length in other books and shall not dwell upon it too long at this time. As I have said in these other books, each of us is the One, each of us is made in the likeness of God, each is the whole, a microcosm. In other words, we are not part of some greater whole, we are not bathed in some cosmic or higher consciousness. Each is the whole. Our problem is that we are seeking to grasp this wholeness as an experience. In the Christian tradition this is what is called *idolatry*. The constant promise that we can soon grasp God, or grasp wholeness—that we can know it as an experience—is what provides much of the motivating power of life. We translate this promise as the promise of success, of power, of getting and gaining, of a supreme love affair, of arcane knowledge, and so on. But beyond all of this is the promise that we shall find ourselves at the center of the world. One writer on mythology put it this way: "The search to be at the center is the nostalgia for paradise. By this we mean to find ourselves always and without effort in the center of the world, at the heart of reality; and by a short cut and in a natural manner to transcend the human condition and to recover the divine condition—as the Christians would say, the condition before the fall."[6]

SLOTH

When the promise seems about to be fulfilled, we are filled with immense energy and determination. We seem to live in the light and are buoyant and joyful. On the other hand, when the promise seems to be a mockery, impossible to realize, we feel a failure, let down, depressed. We seem to be in the dark and lacking in energy and determination. This condition St. John calls spiritual sloth, and he says, "With spiritual sloth beginners are apt to be irked by the things that are the most spiritual, from which they flee because things are incompatible with sensible pleasure. Once they fail to find in prayer the satisfaction that their taste required, they would prefer not to return to it: sometimes they leave it out; other times they continue to do it unwillingly."

How often one hears of people who start Zen practice feeling that at last through Zen they will be able to find their hearts' desire and so are full of energy and determination, but who after a while turn away from the practice or continue doing it in a desultory fashion, saying that it is a waste of time and gives no result, that it is too difficult, or that they have no energy left.

THE DIFFERENCE BETWEEN SPIRITUAL AND PSYCHOLOGICAL DARK NIGHT OF THE SOUL

One question I am sure you will ask is, "How does one know whether the dark night of the soul comes from spiritual or from psychological causes?" Generally speaking, the most common feeling that one has at the onset of the dark night of the soul is a feeling of dryness. It is worth noting that many religions speak of the necessity to pass time in the desert, remember, for example, the temptations of Christ in the desert. Another feeling that often alternates with dryness is a feeling of depression, of the world having lost its savor. One often feels lonely and out of touch with others, even those whom one may love deeply. It not infrequently happens that people who have good marriages, family, and friends nevertheless are filled with a profound loneliness. Later a feeling of anxiety or dread can pervade one's whole life, and one is totally at a loss about how to proceed. Often people abandon their practice at this stage.

As dryness is the most common feeling, let us comment a little more on it and return later to the other, deeper, and in a way more troubling experiences. Not all dryness comes from the dark night, and St. John gives three criteria by which one can determine whether the dryness does indeed come from that or whether it comes "from imperfections or from weakness and lukewarmness or from some bad humor or indisposition of the body."

The first criterion is whether "the soul not only finds no pleasure or consolation in the things of God but also fails to find it in any created thing." Many people find practice too hard or too difficult because other things are calling them and taking up their time and attention. One of the questions that is frequently asked is, Why does it take so long to come to awakening? The answer is very simple: we want something else more than we want awakening. Therefore, if a person finds practice too difficult because he or she spends most of his or her time thinking about playing tennis, fishing, or doing some hobby or other, we can be quite sure that the dryness does not have a spiritual origin. As St. John says with the dark night, "God allows the soul not to find attraction in anything whatsoever." . In other words, the person finds no attraction in life; *everything* is slightly pointless; one is going through the motions but unsure of why.

The second criterion is whether one nevertheless continues to think about the practice, wonder about it, care about it—"whether the memory is centered upon God with painful care and solicitude, thinking that it is not serving God but is backsliding because it finds itself without sweetness in the things of God." Many people come to dokusan complaining about being unable to get on in the practice, but at the same time they are concerned about it, concerned that they are not doing enough, asking how they can deepen the practice, how they can find more time, and so on. This is a sure sign that their need is genuine and that their complaints come from their being adrift in the desert.

One question I often ask if people complain about the practice is, "Why don't you give it up?" For the person who has no real interest, this is the kind of question they have been waiting for! Soon after, they are quite likely to do just that. Others, those who are complaining but whose need is deep, shy away from the question. It would be something like asking a woman who is complaining about the work involved in caring for a child, "Why don't you give the child away?" There is, as St. John says, "a great difference between aridity and lukewarmness."

64

One of the most difficult things about practice is to realize that the practice has nothing to offer the personality. In St. John's words, "The sensual part has no capacity for what is pure spirit; thus, when it is the spirit that receives the pleasure, the flesh is left without savor and is too weak to perform any action." In our age in which personality is king—in which everything is done to give "me" a feeling of importance, of self-esteem, in which the question is no longer whether something is right or wrong but rather whether "I" feel good about it—to follow a practice that has nothing for the personality seems crazy. Such a practice is like swimming against the stream, and this makes the dark night doubly difficult to bear.

The third criterion deals with something that is even more difficult to bear, particularly for those who have enjoyed up until then quite a full and dramatic practice with plenty of insights, deep and changing feelings, flashes of unity, and so on. And this is that the person can no longer meditate as before. Everything seems to dry up. "The soul can no longer meditate or reflect in the imaginative sphere of sense as it was wont, however much it may endeavor to do so. God now begins to communicate Himself to it no longer through the sense as He did aforetime by means of reflections, which joined and sundered its knowledge, but by pure spirit into which consecutive reflections enter not, but he communicates himself to it by an act of simple contemplation." This is the true onset of the dark night. The very practice makes no sense because we have been used to some intellectual, emotional, or imaginative content and accompaniment to our meditations. An intellectual person, particularly one who has enjoyed playing with ideas for their own sake, who knows the sharp sweetness and purity of an intellectual insight, who has seen separate ideas suddenly coalesce and become a greater, broader, deeper understanding, finds that kind of practice, which is "an act of simple contemplation," almost impossible to endure.

HOW TO NAVIGATE THROUGH THE DARK NIGHT

When people who are on the Way find it very painful, it is

often not only because of the dryness itself but also because of the fear that they have strayed from the path, that they have taken a wrong turn, or that the spiritual life is closed to them, "thinking that all spiritual blessings is over for them and that God has abandoned them since they find no help or pleasure in good things, then they grow weary and endeavor (as they have been accustomed to) to concentrate their faculties with some degree of pleasure upon some object of meditation, thinking that when they are not doing this and yet are conscious of making an effort, they are doing nothing. This effort they make not without great inward repugnance and unwillingness on the part of their soul, which was taking pleasure in being at quietness and ease instead of working with its faculties. So they have abandoned one pursuit, yet draw no profit from another."

St. John goes on to say, "They fatigue and overwork their nature, imagining that they are failing through negligence or sin. But this trouble that they are taking is quite useless if God is now leading them by another road, which is that of contemplation and is very different from the first; for the one is of meditation and reasoning, and the other belongs neither to imagination nor yet to reason." Then he says that if "those souls to whom this comes to pass knew how to be quiet at this time and troubled not about performing any action, whether inward or outward, nor had any anxiety about doing anything, then they would delicately experience this inward refreshment in that ease and freedom from care."

In our introduction to Zen we often point out that we use the word *zazen*, rather than the word *meditation*, to describe what we do, because meditation is but one dimension of Zen practice. The other two dimensions are "concentration" and "contemplation." The word *meditate* comes from the Latin *meditari*, "to think about, consider, reflect." A good way to meditate is to take a book written by a someone spiritually mature and read a few lines, and then ponder on what is said—not so much to understand as to enter into the spirit of what is being said. To concentrate means "to direct or draw toward a common center; to focus." Normally this requires considerable mental effort. The word *contemplate* is associated with the word *temple,* which originally was an "open place for observation." Contemplation requires all the freedom that comes with meditation and all the tautness and firmness that is associated with concentration. Contemplation is the heart of practice. Concentration and meditation give support and aid. When we meditate, it is like rain on a parched land; when we concentrate, we generate great energy against which thoughts beat in vain. But contemplation is pure atonement, without goal, effort, or fear of any kind. When we are passing through the dark night, we must use all that is available to us; but staying with the dryness, being one with it however much it might scorch, is the true way.

Two Dark Nights

St. John points out that we must pass through not one but two "dark nights" if we "aspire to the state of perfection." He says the second is a darker and more terrible purgation.

Something similar could be said about Zen practice in that two main stages are encountered: the first ends with kensho, the second with the complete attrition of the ego. The distinction that St. John makes is the first dark night purges the soul of its sensual part, and the second is the purgation of the spiritual part of the soul. In Zen practice a first crucial point is reached when we realize that no experience of any kind is going to give the kind of satisfaction that we crave so deeply. Associated with this realization is the recognition that we suffer because we are human and not because of our parents or our upbringing. This can bring with it not only an insight into our own responsibility for our state but also a recognition of our lack of strength to do anything about it. The second purification occurs after seeing into the truth that one is beyond all form.

St. John gives three reasons why we can speak of the journey of the soul to ultimate union with God as a dark night. The first is that to journey on the way, it is necessary to free ourselves of all those things of the world that we possess; to do this

we must free ourselves of the desire for them. This denial is as a
night to the mind of the human being. The second reason refers
to the journey itself. To make this journey, we must have great
faith, a faith that is like the dark night to human reason and
understanding. The third reason is that the goal itself, God himself, is like a dark night to the soul. However, as St. John points
out, these three are not separate but in truth are all of one
night. He likens it to the night we pass through after the daytime. The first part is comparable to evening going on into
darkness; the second to midnight, the darkest time of all; and
the third is like the end of night or early dawn, which is close
to the light of day, close to divine light. The primary causes of
this night are desire and attachment.

THE FIRST DARK NIGHT OF THE SOUL IS THE NIGHT OF
RELINQUISHING DESIRE

"The quelling of desire may be called a dark night of the soul,
since the soul remains in darkness and without any object
when it is deprived of the pleasure derived from its desire of
things." We must clearly understand what is at issue when St.
John speaks of "quelling" desires. First we must distinguish
between "desire" and "need." We have certain needs, such as
the need for food, sexual activity, shelter, companionship, and
so on. Some people have these needs very strongly, while others
have one or another to a very limited extent. This is due to the
temperament of the person. Many systems insist upon the eradication (where possible) or strict control (where eradication is
not possible) of these needs. These systems are very often established by those having very weak needs and for whom this kind
of work causes very little distress. However, this kind of work
is, as a zen master said, "Like stealing a bell by muffling the
ears." A story in Zen bears upon this point. A master came
across a monk engaged in ascetic practices. He asked the monk,
"Tell me, if a horse and cart won't go, would you flog the horse
or the cart?"

The problematic desires are the ones for fame, power,
acquisition—in short, our desire to find the absolute in

experience. Furthermore, it is not even the desire that is at fault, because fundamentally all desires derive from the desire for unity. All desires come from a basic hunger. As Christ said, they who have this desire are blessed. To use his exact words, "Blessed are they who hunger and thirst after righteousness, for they shall be filled." So it is not the desire but what we do with it, what we invest it in, that is the problem. Everyone is trying to get home, but so many go off into byways, get stuck in cul-de-sacs, try to batter their way out of blind alleys. It is the *objects* of desire that are the problem. No, not even the objects of desire but our making them into something absolute, making them into an idol. This is the problem.

These idols have become beacons beckoning us. Tomorrow, always tomorrow, a new day will dawn. But, as St. John says, the deprivation of objects of desire can be likened to night because in this night no beacon shines. The objects of desire can no longer be seen, although the sense of sight is still active but now without object. When you see that no experience—nothing that can be known, felt, seen, or understood; no amount of fame, riches, love relations, or power; no idol in any shape or form—can satisfy that deep hunger, then you enter into this darkness. St. John is not talking about giving up "things," because, as he says, such an external deprivation—if a desire for those things persists—is not true detachment. The detachment he speaks of leaves one "free and void of things," although one may still have them. "What possesses and harms the soul is not the things of this world but rather the will and desire for them." And it is not the will and desire in themselves but the will and desire for *something*. When we free the will from its bondage to things, it becomes free to hunger and thirst after righteousness.

As long as we have our attention focused upon *something*, it is not free and cannot therefore encompass the whole. "All affection," says St. John, "that the soul has for creatures are pure darkness in the eyes of God." He points out that what we are attracted to we become like. Love creates a likeness between the lover and what is loved. Indeed, the lover is lower than what is loved because he is dependent upon the object of his love. This is why the soul that loves anything (aside from God) renders itself incapable of pure divine union and of transformation in God.

In Zen a similar understanding exists in that we constantly seek to be *something*. Just as St. John says, "Compared with God, all things of earth and heaven are nothing," so it is said in Zen, "When thoughts of the *dharma* are strong, thoughts of the world are weak. But when thoughts of the dharma are weak, thoughts of the world are strong." In the face of wholeness, all parts lose their identity, nothing stands out, nothing exists; but if we give our mind to one thing, be it as small as a speck of dust, wholeness fades into the background. Whatever we claim to be is a "something" when judged against the background of the whole. According to St. John, "Those alone can attain to the wisdom of God who, like ignorant children, lay aside their knowledge and walk in his service with love." Time and again in Zen it is said that all our cleverness, all our understanding, means nothing in the face of the work of the spirit.

THE SECOND DARK NIGHT OF THE SOUL COMES AFTER AWAKENING

It comes as a surprise to many people to hear of a second dark night because they feel that awakening has to be all or nothing. In one way it is. That is to say, if one is awakened, that awakening is not different in any way from the awakening of the Buddhas and the patriarchs. But on the other hand, it is not all or nothing because, as Zen master Kuei-shan says, "The inertia of habit still lingers. This habit has been formed since the beginning of time and cannot be completely banished in one go."

St. John says that the purgation of the senses only becomes fully effective when the purgation of the spirit begins in earnest. It is during this second night that "God will denude the faculties, affections, and feelings—both spiritual and sensual, external, and internal—leaving the understanding in darkness, the will in dryness, and the memory in emptiness; filling the affections of the soul with deepest sadness, bitterness, and tribulations." On the surface this would all seem to be completely negative, but on the contrary, St. John says that this dark night is *an inflowing of God* into the soul, it is infused contemplation whereby God mysteriously teaches the soul the perfection of love without its performing, or even understanding the nature of, the infused contemplation. What produces such striking effects in the soul is the loving wisdom of God, the purifying and illuminating action of which prepares the soul for the union of love with God.

Before awakening, one tends to take the personality for granted; one *is* the personality; one is one's life. Awakening breaks this identification. If it is very deep, the subsequent work is relatively fast. But for most of us, the initial awakening is shallow, and so the work can be hard and long. Joshu, one of the greatest of Zen masters, stayed with his teacher of forty years after his awakening, and even then, after his teacher had died, he went on a pilgrimage for twenty years seeking further purification. This subsequent purification can be called a dark night because with the break in identification, we see clearly the contradictions inherent in the personality and the many stratagems, tricks, and follies we have used both to hide these contradictions from ourselves and others and to cope with the extreme pain that they can give. Seeing the personality in this way—against the background of purity and freedom—gives rise to a feeling of profound shame, remorse, and sadness; as St. John says, the soul is filled "with deepest sadness, bitterness, and tribulations."

Let me conclude with the Admonition of Kuei-shan, an admonition well known in Zen circles:

> If one is truly awakened and has realized the fundamental, and is aware of it oneself, in such a case one is actually no longer tied to the poles of practice. But normally, even though the original mind has been awakened through practice, so that one is instantaneously awakened to knowing, the inertia of habit still lingers. This habit has been formed since the beginning of time and cannot be completely banished in one go. One must therefore be

taught to cut off completely the stream of one's habitual ideas and views that are held in place by unresolved karma. This process of purification is practice. I don't say that one must follow a hard-and-fast method. One need only be taught the general direction that this purification must take.

What you hear must first be accepted by your reason; and when your rational mind is deepened and made subtle in an ineffable way, your mind will of its own become spontaneously understanding and bright, never to fall back into a state of doubt and confusion. However numerous and varied are the subtle teachings, one will know intuitively how to apply them—which to hold back and which to use—according to the needs of the occasion. Only in this way will you be qualified to sit in the chair and wear your robe as a master of the true art of living.

To sum up, it is of utmost importance to know that ultimate reality, the foundation of pure knowing, does not admit of a single speck of dust; nevertheless, in the innumerable paths of action, not a single law is to be broken nor thing to be abandoned. When you can break through with a single stroke of the sword without much ado, then all discrimination between sacred and the profane is annihilated once and for all, and your whole being reveals true eternity in which reigns the nonduality of one knowing and the myriad particular things.

—·—·—·—·—·—·—·—·—·—·—·—·—·—·—·—·—·—

Take care that you always choose
Not the easiest, but the hardest;
Not the most delectable, but the most distasteful;
Not what gives you most pleasure, but what is least
pleasing;
Not what allows you much rest, but what requires great
exertion;
Not what consoles you, but what deprives you of consolation;
Not the loftiest and the most precious, but the lowest
and the most despised;

72

Not the desire for anything, but the desire for nothing.
Do not go about seeking the best of temporal things, but the worst.
Desire nothing but to enter for Christ's sake into total nakedness, emptiness,
and poverty with respect to all the things of this world.

—St. John

CHAPTER SEVEN

A Little Boy Goes to Heaven

A little boy knocked on the gates of heaven, and when St. Peter came to the gate, the boy asked to be allowed in. St. Peter asked him to wait while he went to consult with God. While waiting the boy looked around at the vast and wide landscape that surrounded him. The season being late autumn, the trees were covered with leaves: gold, crimson, orange, and green. As far as the eye could see blazed trees upon trees, hills upon hills of flaming beauty.

St. Peter returned. "I have God's answer. Do you see all those trees?" and he swept his hand around the full 360 degrees of the horizon. The little boy replied, "Yes." Peter went on, "God said that when the leaves have fallen from those trees as many times as there are leaves on the trees, you may come into heaven."

The little boy sat down without haste and, looking up to St. Peter, said, "Please tell God the first leaf has fallen."

It is a condition of complete simplicity
(Costing not less than everything.)

PART 3

Dharma Talks

CHAPTER EIGHT

Know Yourself!

Dogen says, "To practice Zen is to know the self. To know the self is to forget the self."

What does it mean, "To practice Zen is to know the self"?

As a rule we do not know the self; instead, we know things, thoughts, emotions, feelings—but not the self. When Gurdjieff says *we do not remember ourselves,* he is saying much the same thing as Dogen does.

But is not the trouble that we are too full of the self?

Yes, but we forget what is essential. Dogen says that to know the self is to forget the self, but before we can forget the self, we must know the self. We constantly use the word "I." All our conversations, real and imaginary, revolve around "I." We say, "I" like and "I" don't like; "I" want and "I" don't want. We confuse "I" with the self; although they cannot be separated, they are not the same. A Zen nun said, "I cannot pull out the weed because if I do so, I'll pull out the flower." A Zen master said something similar when he said, "The thief my son!" It is like a mirror and its reflections: they are not two, yet they are not the same. "I" too is a reflection, a reflection with which we are quite fascinated, evoking as it does a constant and unending drama of emotions, fears and failures, successes and joys. We ride the surf of life on the board of "I," struggling to stay on the crest but forever plunging into waves of distress. "I" is always something that is going to happen in the future, something to look forward to, to achieve, to get, to win. From this comes the ride's momentum.

The satisfaction of "I" is our cult; to this we bend our will and desire. Ego, like a dead king, has to be nourished, satisfied at all costs—so much so that we frequently confuse ego satisfaction with happiness, even though they differ as much as sand and rice. Intense ego satisfaction can often be found hand in hand with profound unhappiness. One only has to think of rock stars clutching, straining at the microphone in a daze of light and stupor while basking in the adulation of strangers, or of harried executives treading like donkeys the wheel of public acclaim, wearied by long nights, hotel rooms, and airports, worn by the burden of their very success. On the other hand, although perhaps more rarely, happiness comes without any ego satisfaction. Monks, hermits, and anchorites sometimes find this kind of happiness, but so do men and women who are simply content with what they have, regardless of whether it is much or little.

Ego satisfaction is a clear reflection of self, or as clear as the muddy water of experience will allow. We are always searching for it, and when we find it we cherish, guard, and seek to perpetuate it, even at the cost of health, sanity, and sometimes life itself. It has many degrees and gradations. For example, *the sensation of self,* the most basic of all self-reflections, provides the most elementary ego satisfaction. When we are uncertain, undecided, embarrassed, or have stage fright, we lose the sensation of self. We sometimes say after an embarrassing moment, "I was completely at sea," "I was lost," "I was out of my mind," and so on. If the uncertainty is great, then feelings of anxiety, fear, or panic can flood in. So we develop strategies to cope with the anxiety by restoring the sensation of self. Men stroke their chins, using the stubble as a kind of sandpaper. Women touch their hair. We touch our noses, lick our lips, cross our arms or legs (or both). All to restore the sensation of the self.

All this is very innocuous. But some people hurt themselves, even stab themselves, to recover this lost sensation. I remember seeing a young girl walking along a street holding on to her mother with one hand. Her other arm flailed up and down against her side, punishing her hip. Whip, whip, whip, the arm never stopped, except when the street was so crowded that the arm was obstructed. And then the girl looked around like someone drowning, panicky, until she had managed to force her way back through the crowd into a free area beyond, where the arm was able to continue its brutal work.

We have yet another deeper, more subtle, strategy for gaining the sensation of self. This is through tension, physical tension. Most people are like Gothic cathedrals of tension: each tension holds in place other tensions, which in turn hold others in their place. The keystone is "I," and like a little boy running downhill to keep his balance, we are all running after this keystone that holds in place the arch of our existence. Sometimes when people meditate, they let go of this keystone for a moment—and the whole structure moves, subsides, slides. This movement creates great fear and uncertainty, calling for more tension, gritting of teeth, clenching of fists, holding of diaphragms, bearing down on the back of necks.

Beyond the strategy of tension lies another that depends upon a habitual emotion, such as dull anxiety, vague depression, smoldering rage. We poke the fires of negativity with memories: past failures, past conflicts, past betrayals and humiliations. Constantly we rake the coals, seeking to know the self in the light and heat of their pain. The last thing people abandon, said Gurdjieff, is their suffering. For many, the goal of their life—the final keystone—is to free themselves of a certain kind of anxiety, a certain kind of pain; but if they were to do so, their life would lose its meaning, and so the vicious cycle is maintained.

Deeper still is the monologue, that unending discussion with the Other hidden in the twilight of our minds. Cajoling, explaining, lecturing, arguing, the discussion is endless. Central to it all is the hope for the final enthronement of "I." Many conversations with friends and enemies are simply continuations of this monologue; then the Other emerges from the gloom and for a moment stands before us. After a while the conversation ends, the light goes out, but the monologue goes on. It goes on even in sleep, where it becomes inextricably woven with images into dreams. Plans, projects, and goals harness the energy otherwise dissipated by the monologue, but even so the plans, the goals, are still part of this soap opera in which I am the director, the producer, the star performer, and the audience. Others, friends and enemies alike, are the supporting cast and must know their roles, speak their lines, enter and exit on cue. If they miss their lines, change them, act out of character, we say that life is full of accidents, injustice, failures and that others are unfair, irresponsible, unfeeling. We judge ourselves and others, apportion blame and praise, all according to the script of our life's drama. Did not Shakespeare say that all the world's a stage and all the men and women merely players?

When I am told we must know ourselves, I think it means knowing about the star of the soap opera, what molded him, where he learned his roles or how he came to speak these lines. We think that to know means to analyze, to find cause and effect, to see seeds being planted and harvests reaped—seeds of loneliness, anger, cruelty, fear, and anxiety; harvests of misery, failure, despair. We trace the flourishing of the seeds as weeds and wonder at the sun and rain, the situations that must have fertilized them, and so try to get to know this garden in which flowers, weeds, grass, and thorns all strive in a symbiosis we call the personality.

This, however, is not what Dogen means when he talks about knowing the self, nor what Gurdjieff means by "remembering the self." To know the self requires that we take a first step and see the drama, regardless of content, as a drama, and know it to be a reflection. Few are able to take this first necessary step, because we are so convinced the drama is real, that the props and cast, the scenes and dialogue, are real, having a life independent of what we put in. Nowadays this conviction of the reality of the drama has even reached the point where we are all victims: women are victims, workers are victims, patients are victims, citizens are victims. We complain, protest, litigate, all in the solid conviction that it is "they" who are the cause, that "it" is the problem.

We take it all so completely for granted.

When I was young the film industry was also young. It was a time when the Western was popular. I remember once seeing a film about a sheriff in a white hat, on a white horse, with a gun in a white holster, who was riding into town for a showdown with an outlaw who, of course, had a black hat, a black horse, a black mustache, and a black gun. The sheriff rode upright, tall in the saddle, into town to confront the bad guy standing in the middle of the road, slightly crouched, waiting for him to get off his horse so the gun duel could begin.

The sheriff rode slowly down the wide road flanked by saloons and stores. The road was empty apart from the lone outlaw, behind whom, and stretching into the far distance, lay the vast, desolate desert punctuated by cacti and rocks. Beyond the desert rose up, blue and purple, snow-peaked mountains.

The tension mounts as the lawman approaches the showdown. He reins in his horse, gets down, and with his back turned carelessly to the outlaw, hitches the horse to a nearby post. Without any haste at all he turns and surveys the scene. The tension is turned up another notch. Who will make the first move? Everything seems frozen in eternity for a few moments. Then the mountains move! Not by much, but they moved! They are not real; they are simply painted on a huge canvas. In a moment the whole thing—cowboys, desert, horses, saloons—becomes a farce. You can't take it seriously anymore. Who cares who shoots whom? It is no longer real but just an illusion that I make real for my own amusement.

To know the self, we must make the mountains move. All we need is just an insight—not much, just a flash, a moment in which no reflection occurs.

These moments go on all the time, and all the time we close up against them. We close up against a loss of self, we react, we clench, we adopt one strategy or another. The resistance is almost instinctive. This is why all religions tell us to watch, to be alert and mindful, to be present so that when these moments happen, we can allow them just to happen without the resistance. Indeed, one cannot help wondering whether this is what Christ was referring to with his parable of the wise and foolish virgins. At the end of the parable the bridegroom came, and those who were ready went in with him to the marriage feast; and the door was shut. "Afterward the foolish virgins came also saying, 'Lord, lord open to us.' But he replied, 'Truly I say to you I do not know you.' Watch therefore, for you know neither the day nor the hour."

This moment of nonreflection unveils the awakening before the awakening, the moment when *bodhichitta* arises. An awakening upstream of reflection, upstream of all conflict in a moment of knowing without content, without any awareness of knowing. One cannot even speak of "a moment of knowing." Knowing shines. Dogen calls this knowing "forgetting the self." Bodhidharma calls it nonknowing in reply to the question put to him by Emperor Wu, "Are you not a holy man?"

The counterpart to pure knowing may be called peace or even bliss, a peace or bliss not that one feels but rather that one knows; knowing is bliss. It might well be what the New Testament calls a peace that "passes understanding." However, to those who are used to knowing the self through a curtain of suffering and conflict, this peace yawns as a threat, an abyss, a source of dread. Only those who can be present see it as an opportunity for a turnabout, *pravritti,* as it is known in Sanskrit. With this turnabout the lusting after reflection, the search to grasp the absolute in transitory experience, loses its grip. One no longer experiences things as objective and independent, but as reflections within knowing. Upstream of all necessity to focus attention, all conflict becomes a dance, all opposition melts as "I" and the Other are known as two faces of one reality. The preparation for this turnabout often takes a long time; it is what Zen practice is all about.

But someone may well object, saying that focusing the attention, concentrating, is also what the practice is all about. Yes, sometimes practice does call for intense concentration requiring intense effort, even physical effort. This allows the mind to withdraw from all the petty foci that obstruct it. If we focus the mind intensely, we can break the thousands of threads that tie us down as the threads of the Lilliputians tied down Gulliver. But then we must go beyond that effort. Although concentration and force of mind has its place, practice goes far beyond it in contemplation. Contemplation means "being one with," being completely open. In this lies the great difference between practicing with a koan and practicing with a mantra. To practice with a koan, one must keep the mind open. Zen masters have called it the *doubt sensation*. On the other hand, the mantra has the effect of closing the mind, of giving it a permanent focus. The doubt sensation, also called the yearning sensation or the longing sensation, allows the mind to become more and more aroused without its resting on anything, to the point where pure awareness without content, reflection, or desire can spring forth in a burst of light, in an explosion of pure being. The turnabout must be sudden; it is as though one makes a leap from something to nothing, or better still from something to everything.

TWO WAYS OF PRACTICE

The only way to know yourself is to be, which means to forget all that you think you are. God says somewhere, "Be still and know that I am God." This is what we mean by simply "be." God's statement could easily, without loss, be reduced to "Be still and know" or just "Be still" or, as we have just said, "Be." Being is knowing; knowing is stillness; and this still knowing, which is being without limit, some people call God. Meister Eckehart the great German Christian mystic says, "God makes us to know him, and his knowing is being, and his making me to know him is the same as my knowing, so his knowing is mine." But to be able to enter into the stillness that is one's own true nature, one must break up constantly the addiction and fascination with being *something*. This is why it is said that the practice has two directions: one toward arousing the mind without resting it upon anything, the other toward dissolving all the identities we have created over the millennia.

We use the word *dissolving* quite deliberately because awareness is itself a solvent. Simply allowing a thought, idea, anxiety, or compulsion to rest within the field of awareness dissolves that thought, idea, and so on. In a way the effectiveness of some psychotherapy depends upon the dissolving power of awareness. Allowing people to talk about their concerns encourages them to experience those concerns fully. Getting someone to pinpoint what it is that is worrying him or her in itself often releases him or her from the worry. However, no judgment whatever should intervene. From this point of view, a psychotherapy that does not have a heavily structured philosophy underlying it is more effective than one that comes out of a specific theory of the mind. In the former case the therapist more readily accepts without any kind of judgment what the client has to say, whereas the therapist who relies on a theory, at some level or another, looks for what the client has to say that corresponds to the theory.

Most of us find sitting without judgment, not wanting to change a painful state, not trying to get to a state of complete peace, very difficult, and we can only do so after practice, sometimes very long practice. As one sits in this way, many different kinds of experiences surge up in the mind: strange thoughts and ideas—sometimes cruel, violent, lustful, or shameful. Some are quite antisocial and would be quite unacceptable to others, were one to discuss them. But even so, we must allow them to be, must let them float in awareness. Sometimes it feels as though one is surely committing spiritual suicide. It feels that all that is best in one's life is being eroded and lost. But still go on. This is faith. An all-merciful God need not forgive us our sins, nor need a priest give us absolution. True confession means just what I am describing. An all-merciful father, the intercession of the Virgin Mary, the power of a priest to forgive, all focus the natural healing power of awareness, the natural tendency for wholeness to rediscover itself.

I was brought up in a very poor area of London and, at one time, was friendly with a doctor and would sometimes accompany him on his rounds because, in those days, doctors would make house calls. One day I asked him how he treated people who might have psychological problems that they had converted into physical maladies. These people were too poor to pay for any extended treatment, or even for medication. He smiled and said that he always used the latest wonder drug. I asked him what he meant. He pulled out a bottle of different-colored pills. "These are just sugar pills," he said, "but when I find people whose problems have a psychological rather than a physical base, I give them some of these pills. I always tell them that they are very lucky because research had just come up with exactly the right treatment for their particular problem. I say that the pills are really very, very expensive, but it so happens that I have been given some as samples and that they can therefore have them without cost. It is amazing how often people recover, sometimes from problems that can have alarming physical symptoms."

Healing is always done by the mind, by awareness acting as a solvent. When we cut our hand, it heals; that is, it becomes whole again. When we cut the mind through separation, it too can heal and so become whole. Medicines help; sometimes they are essential. But it is still the mind that heals.

When sitting, one should not go on a fishing expedition trying to get the mind to throw up its debris. Sitting even as the tensions arise, even as agitation and feelings of discomfort and malaise enter in, without trying to add something or take anything away, allows the mind gradually to heal itself, to become whole again.

Pure awareness without reflection may be likened to a smooth sheet of paper. If one were to make a crease down the center, the surface of one part can reflect the surface of another part. The mind of an adult resembles a paper ball that has been crumpled up and in which all the different surfaces of the paper reflect all the other surfaces, and out of all this comes a dissonance, a cacophony, just noise. But as one sits, so one allows the paper gradually to smooth out. As it does so, the wrinkles drop away, and more and more, harmony reappears and wholeness returns and makes itself known.

Underlying all our suffering is wholeness. Indeed, we suffer because we are whole. Once we can truly see this, then the mark of our pain is the mark of our wholeness and can change our attitude to both the pain and the work we do on ourselves. We should not consider ourselves to be fragmented and having to collect ourselves together. We are whole, one sheet of paper, but wholeness is masked and lost sight of in the crisscross of experience. We must allow wholeness to manifest itself. Wholeness will ultimately assert itself whether or not you practice Zen. Wholeness is basic reality and will ultimately make itself known. Indeed, because of this, *because* wholeness is asserting itself, you are working on yourself. Wholeness asserting itself is not the cause while working on yourself, that is sitting in zazen, the effect. Wholeness asserting itself is "working on yourself," it is "doing zazen." Because of this, because wholeness is asserting itself, you are working on yourself and the paper is smoothing out. You are practicing Zen. But when all is said and done, *you* are not practicing Zen; it is simply wholeness that is making itself known. Resistance to practice comes from "me" practicing, "me" trying to divert the practice into making "me" happy, getting "me" free from pain, "I" want to come to awakening, and so practice is hard and dry and difficult.

It is from wholeness making itself known that the hunger and thirst we feel in practice originates. This is why the Christian mystic said, "Do not quench your thirst." It is also why a Zen master in reply to a monk who asked him "Where is my treasure?" said, "Your question is your treasure." A great difference exists between this natural hunger and an ambition to come to awakening. This hunger cannot be frustrated; it is not in a hurry. It has no images or thoughts to bolster it. It has immense power but requires no physical effort. Lacking in drama, it is often accompanied by the feeling that nothing is happening. Indeed, at a superficial level, because we are so used to having some clear ideas about where we are and where we want to go, it may well be accompanied by the feeling that we have lost our way.

As this hunger increases it undermines our very orientation. Everything that one knows, all the values that one has, all the meaning that one has found, all of this is but a reflection and must be called into question. When the true light begins to shine, all gets lost among the shadows. But do not be afraid. If you let go of all the shadows, the light will shine clear and unobstructed.

Nisargadatta said on one occasion, "See how you function. Watch the motives and the results of your actions. Study the prison you have built around yourself by inadvertence. By knowing what you are not, you come to know yourself. The way back to yourself is through discernment."

"The way back to yourself is through discernment." Gurdjieff uses the expression "to separate the coarse from the fine," which is a good, concrete way of talking about discernment. Of course, you cannot separate yourself from the reflective mind, any more than you can separate a reflection from a mirror. But through discernment, you can see clearly that the reflection is not the mirror, that you are not the reflective mind. When you have allowed the conflicts, antagonisms, and frustrations of the reflective mind and its contents to dissolve within pure awareness, when you have allowed them simply to be there, then a moment of clarity, of true discernment, is possible. At this moment of true discernment, one knows the self, yet one has forgotten the self.

— · — · — · — · — · — · — · — · — · — · — · — · —

> Truly, truly, I say to you, unless a grain of wheat falls
> into the earth and dies, it remains alone; but if it dies, it
> bears much fruit. The one who loves his life loses it, and
> he who turns aside from life in this world shall keep it
> for eternal life.

— · — · — · — · — · — · — · — · — · — · — · — · —

The Mountain of Inertia

*Jesus said, "If two make peace with one another in the
same house,
They will say to the mountain,
'Move!' and it will move"*

—The Gospel of Thomas

The great enemy of Zen practice is inertia, the disease of
"tomorrow." "Tomorrow I'll feel more like it," "Tomorrow
I'll have more time," "Tomorrow I'll not be so tired, shall not be
so rushed, shall not have this, shall not have that." Tomorrow. Ah!
tomorrow, the great labor-saving device. Tomorrow is freedom;
it is pure potential, pure possibility. Tomorrow is like a bright
blue sky. The only problem is that it is always tomorrow. As the
dormouse said to Alice, "Jam tomorrow, why is it always jam
tomorrow and never jam today?"

Because, of course, today we must work for it and not just
hope.

The only reason to practice Zen is . . . there is no reason.
This is the problem. To motivate people is to show them that
they—or others, or the future, or at least something—will benefit in some way from what they are doing. Give me a reason
and I'll move the earth. What about "No reason"?

Our practice has nothing for the ego; how can it when it

is the very clinging to something that is our obstacle, this same clinging that, after all, forms the basis of the ego? All our values relate back to this clinging, give reasons and justifications for it. All our hopes are in its support; all our fears are in its demise. "Am I or am I not?" The great debate, which gains in favor of "I am not" with the steady, relentless march of time. To be something, anything, so long as I can be it forever; to be something absolutely, so that no doubt, no insecurity, no threat, comes from outside or inside. The ultimate security. The ultimate security is the ultimate inertia. It won't budge. A mighty fortress is our God, but a mighty mountain is our inertia. Immortal, invincible, a rock of ages, omniscient, omnipotent, the ultimate, the absolute, the prime mover unmoved: so have we created our God in our own image or in the image of how we should like to be. And so we hang in there.

So why work? Why struggle with a practice that gives no reward? Do you remember when Emperor Wu asked Bodhidharma, "What is the merit for all my good actions?" Bodhidharma replied, "No merit my lord." A young man phoned me up and said, "I have been practicing now for three whole weeks and nothing has happened!" I said, "Congratulations!" He said "Eh? I don't understand. Why congratulations?" I said, "People have been working for this for years, and you have come to it in a mere three weeks." Just imagine, nothing happens. Pure immutable stillness, pure peace. The peace that passes all understanding, all grasping. The peace that is your true nature and on which we have turned our backs and so have to encounter it as reality "out there." True nature, moreover, can seem so threatening, so awful when its face has not been covered over with busyness, action, getting, using, consuming, striving for . . . pure immutable stillness, peace that passes all understanding.

But sitting is so hard, so dry, so painful so . . . let's face it, so boring, so dull. I just go to sleep; or if I don't go to sleep, I just sit there frustrated, tying myself in knots, wondering what the hell I'm supposed to do.

If there is nothing to gain, there is nothing that needs to

be done to gain it. That frustration, that pain, that boredom, are all manifestations of true nature. A story is told of a Zen master who on his deathbed was calling out in pain. The monks were quite embarrassed and asked him how he, a Zen master, could behave so. He said, "My crying out in pain is no different to my cries of joy."

A koan in the Mumonkan tells of a monk, Seizei, who goes to Zen master Sozan and says, "I am poor and destitute, I beg you, feed me." The master called, "Seizei!" and Seizei says, "Yes, master." Sozan says, "There, you have drunk three glasses of the best wine in China and still you say you have not yet moistened your lips."

When we struggle, when we ask, "What must I do?" when we are overcome by inertia and boredom, we are saying, " I am poor and destitute."

Mumon asks, "At what point did Seizei drink the wine?"

_ . _ . _ . _ . _ . _ . _ . _ . _ . _ . _ . _ . _ . _ . _ . _

A monk asked, "How can you tell what is true before the blossoming awakening?"

"It is blossoming now," said the master.

_ . _ . _ . _ . _ . _ . _ . _ . _ . _ . _ . _ . _ . _ . _ . _

Some Thoughts about Practice

Why does one practice Zen? This is an important question for beginners. Whenever someone comes to the Center to inquire about practicing Zen, we always ask him or her, "Why do you want to do that?" We also emphasize this question during workshops; in fact, the first talk given at a workshop is, to a large extent, dedicated to getting the participants to think very seriously about it.

One advantage of doing this is that it brings to light the unrealistic expectations that people have. The need that we have as children to be omniscient and omnipotent, all-knowing and all-powerful, is one that very often persists at a subconscious level of the mind. We expect that in some way these wishes to be omniscient and omnipotent will be fulfilled by Zen practice, that somehow practice will give us powers and capabilities that we feel we ought to have but do not at the moment. Because meditation is often associated with the magical and a belief that it is a way of getting something for nothing, it gets linked to these hidden desires.

These expectations, and the criteria they provide by which to judge our practice, make us dissatisfied with it and with ourselves. By questioning sincerely why we practice, we can undermine those expectations by seeing into them, seeing them for what they are worth. This can relieve us of a great burden. By "seeing into them" I mean to allow whatever to come up, to pass through the pure light of awareness, and so become integrated and part of the harmonious whole. If we could live without expectations, we would never be disappointed. Disappointment is violation of expectations, and much of the despair that people suffer comes from this violation. The etymology of the word *expectation* is *ex,* which means "outside of," and *spectore,* which means "to look." To expect therefore means to look outside of oneself. Expectations turn away from "what is" and toward what will or ought to be. The practice of Zen goes in quite the opposite direction.

Even if you have been practicing for some time it is well to ask yourself this question periodically, particularly when you seem to be stuck and getting nowhere and just up against a wall. Ask yourself, "Why am I doing this? What makes me do this practice?" One of the problems is that after we have practiced for a while, it often becomes a routine, just another thing to do, another way to pass time. It becomes yet one more way to pass our lives in mechanical activities. An important reason for Zen practice is to see into this very mechanicalness, but if practice itself has become one activity among all the others, then it ceases have any value at all. By reminding ourselves of why we practice, we can break through this mechanical practice.

Although to begin with we may have some unrealistic demands, it goes without saying that we can also have some perfectly legitimate reasons for practicing. In the beginning of *An Invitation to Practice Zen,* I suggest several: relief from stress, psychological peace, better concentration, increased creativity. However, if one or other (or more) of these is the only reason, if we look at meditation only in this way, we reduce it to a kind of shopping expedition. When we shop, we often do so in the hope of finding something that will satisfy a hunger. But how often, at the very moment of unwrapping what we have bought, do we taste dust and ashes, realizing that we have done nothing to satisfy our hunger and, if anything, have simply inflamed it? It can be this way too in Zen. It may well happen that we get what we want, but it may equally well happen that we do not want what we get.

Why does one practice? Dwelling on this question, thinking about it, pondering on it, meditating on it, pushing it to its ultimate, you will come to realize that *you do not know* why you practice. But what kind of "I don't know" is this? It does not mean that you are all mixed up and confused because of a lot of conflicting ideas and theories. It is true that some of us *are* like that, but then we should take time off to think things through more carefully. But even so, even after this work, we are still unable truly to formulate or conceptualize why we practice.

This "I don't know" is backed by a powerful drive, by a longing, a yearning. Something basic seems to be missing in life, but we cannot give it a name. On the face of it, we might think "If only I could get a better job, a more loving or understanding partner, live in a different location, things would be better." And so they might, for a while. If we dwell on this lack, it sometimes also seems as though we have in the past taken a wrong path or left something important undone, or some talent unfulfilled. We ache, feel a deep longing, some profound anguish. Asking ourselves why we practice, refusing to accept ready-made clichés, dwelling upon the question—this itself becomes the practice. Very often in workshops we say that the reason we practice is to find out why we're practicing. Although this has a jaunty Zen ring about it, it nevertheless does have some truth.

Martin Heidegger has warned that the great danger of our age is that we can become so fascinated, so delighted, so taken up, with technological thinking that meditative thinking could die out altogether. This is particularly true of the technical thinking that underlies much of the research into the nature of life and of the mind. We are dazzled by the technological capabilities that we have, particularly in the field of computer technology, and the idea that we may be able to see more deeply into life's mysteries by meditation than by calculative thinking is now dismissed without a thought. The belief that we can reduce life's mysteries to a simple formula has seized the imagination of researchers. In fact, one of the ultimate aims in science, according to Stephen Hawking, is to reduce the whole mystery of existence to a formula that you can wear on your T-shirt. However, being open to the mystery of mind, which means to be open to the possibility of knowing yet never being able to say what we know, may well be the most worthwhile endeavor of life.

The extreme emphasis on positivist research and the belief that mysteries are simply badly formulated questions has its counterpart in the growing belief that we are essentially spectators and that the aim in life is to have as many options as possible by which we can observe without being directly affected. We are losing touch with the world of feelings and thoughts, ideas, sensations, urges, desires, and frustrations other than those artificially induced by electronics. For many people, their own mind, with its own desires and feelings, is just unknown territory. When talking with another, it becomes evident whether that person is practicing some spiritual discipline. One can be introduced to a complete stranger and within a short while know whether he or she has had some spiritual training. What she says and the way she says it and the way she conducts herself in relation to others very often has overtones that can only come about through having a richer and deeper understanding of this inner world. With electronic "interaction" these overtones just do not exist.

Thus, it could be said that at least one reason for meditating—although not the most basic—is to get to know our own inner life, its fundamental mystery, as well as to get to know the forces and dynamics that it is made of and to appreciate the hunger and longing that pervades our lives. By meditating we can get to know pain as pain and not as something to be avoided at all costs, and we come to see the limitations within which we have to work. This does not mean we get to know all this in a psychological way, in terms of psychotherapy or psychology or in terms of a structured theory. Instead, we get to see, for example, that we have thoughts, desires, intentions, all in conflict with one another; that we can take up an attitude one day about something and have a completely contradictory attitude the next. We can have this contradictory attitude toward meditation itself. One day we feel that it is something that is truly meaningful in our lives, something very worthwhile, and often we cannot specify what we mean by this; nevertheless, we have a real sense of its value. On another day, we curse it, wish we did not have to be bothered with it, find it a burden, feel that it is completely useless. We have this same contradictory attitude toward many other things, toward other people, toward the work we do, toward life itself. Out of this contradiction come our pain, negative emotions, humiliations, and so on. By knowing these contradictions in this way, we can cease to resist them, cease trying to make them reasonable and trying to justify them to ourselves and others. Being left alone, they have a tendency to find their own pattern and harmony, often canceling each other out, fading in the light of awareness, or simply dropping away as we forgive ourselves.

As Nisargadatta once pointed out, such meditation profoundly affects our character. We are slaves to what we do not know, whereas we are masters of what we do know. Whatever vice or weakness we uncover in ourselves, and whose causes and workings we come to understand, we overcome by the very knowing. The inadvertence dissolves when brought into the light of awareness. Just by opening ourselves, by allowing whatever is to remain in the light of awareness, we rob it of its power to harm. We must open ourselves in this way without any judgment, without any need to integrate, change, or do something else about whatever appears. This is the meditative counterpart to Christ's injunctions "Resist not evil" and "Love your enemies." It is a very difficult practice, particularly when deep anxiety, raging anger, or the feelings of failure and of having wasted our lives are involved. But, nevertheless, if we go in this direction as best we can, not necessarily completely opening ourselves without judgment each time, we find more and more that these painful experiences are all based upon thoughts, that they come out of a warped awareness masking a still deeper pain, which in turn can be transmuted. The very fact of being able to do this, of being able to dissolve painful states in awareness, gives us a new confidence and assurance that we can cope with the complexity of life.

However, sometimes we are taken over by ways of reacting to situations, difficulties, and so on that are extremely destructive. They are so powerful and painful that we cannot simply sit with them. Naturally, we want to change this kind of thing—we want to bring it under control—but the more we struggle, the worse it gets. In this case we should begin with a *wish* that we could just be open to it. A wish has its own kind of power, but unfortunately we have reduced wishes to functions in fairy tales and overlook this power. To wish ardently is a way of praying. A wish comes with a certain kind of dynamic knowing, and to really wish or pray or open yourself to the full possibility is a very profound way of working with this kind of difficulty. If possible, it is best to wish or pray in this way in the presence of, say, a figure of the bodhisattva of compassion or, if you are a Christian, within the presence of a figure of the Virgin Mary. Both are expressions of love—of the profound binding power of unity—that, while transcending all form, nevertheless can be invoked by form for some people. However, when doing so, you should never wish to avoid the consequences of your destructive difficulty, but rather wish to have the strength to pay in full the debt you have incurred by reason of it.

Gurdjieff says that everything begins with a wish. "I wish, I can, I will." This holds true also if you truly wish to practice. Sometimes practice becomes so much of a burden; you just don't know what to do. We can, at such times, wish to practice, to open ourselves, to call on the wider forces we contain, to call on these wider forces of compassion and wisdom to help us to break through these blocks, not by doing away with them but by helping us find the power to sustain them, to be open to them.

I remember times in my own training at Rochester Zen Center when I was lost in darkness, caught in a cul-de-sac that had no exit. I sometimes had no idea of what to do next, whether to sit or run, whether to try or to give up. As Zen master Rinzai said, it was "sheer darkness all over." Next to the zendo was a shrine dedicated to Kannon, the bodhisattva of compassion, and I would sit in this room amid this call of prayer or wish or dynamic meditation—call it what you will— that came not so much from me as from the bodhisattva as the full expression of my need. Just to be in this presence can be very, very useful. If it is not possible to have a bodhisattva, then it's always possible to have a picture. But whatever it is, it can enable you to lend yourself without defining in a clear way what it is that you're lending yourself to. It is really enough to say that you are lending yourself to the forces of good in your common presence, lending yourself to them in the fullest possible way.

Becoming aware of our contradictions, we can see the pain they can create for ourselves and others. At one level, unless we are at home with ourselves to some degree, the practice is going to be extremely difficult. The practice of being open to what is and of wishing to be at home in ourselves, wishing to be one, wishing to be in harmony, can be for most people an extremely important aspect of practice. Even so, from another point of view, all this is still a form of shopping and is secondary to what Zen practice is about.

However, by being at one with ourselves—no matter what the situation—by encompassing the contradictions, by aligning ourselves with the force of unity, the mind becomes quiet, like a clean sheet of paper, as Yasutani Roshi would have called it. "When the mind is quiet," Nisargadatta tells us, "we come to know ourselves as pure witness." This practice is called in Japanese *shikantaza,* which is often translated as "simply sitting." However, we must be careful because we may think we are practicing shikantaza but instead are simply observing the mind within the mirror of the mind, a condition called by the Zen masters "the pit of pseudo-emancipation," or "the cave of demons." Furthermore, what Nisargadatta calls "knowing ourselves as witness" is quite different from *observing,* and the distinction between these two is so important that we must dwell upon it for the moment.

The word *witness* comes from an old English word *wit,* which meant "knowing." This is different from simply being an observer. The mind has two modes of being: one is the mode of participant, and the other is the mode of the observer. These are two contradictory points of view. The point of view of the participant is from within the center outward. The point of view of the observer is outside looking toward the center. These two points of view are equally valid and arise *simultaneously* within a single individual. They are mutually dependent but at the same time mutually antagonistic, and so are potentially at war with each other.

One way by which the war is resolved is by simply becoming pure observer. Those who take this route take on a slightly cynical, sardonic attitude and have a tendency to over-analyze situations, to criticize their situation and themselves very harshly in order to keep things at arm's length. Such people always want to stay dispassionate and uninvolved, and this attitude leads ultimately to a kind of frigid relation both with themselves and with the world. Accompanying this is often a feeling of raging against a wasteland.

The alternative mode is the mode of the participant. These people throw themselves willy-nilly, holus-bolus, into situations. They are always either terribly enthusiastic about things or terribly depressed. Their life is one drama after another. They always wind up ragged, their lives lacking in harmony, and they tend to be very irritable with other people when these others do not get as involved and enthusiastic as they are about things, or when people are not sympathetic toward them when they're depressed, not knowing which way to turn.

These two modes are present to some degree in each of us. It is evident that the "observer mode" encourages a pseudo-Soto approach in that Soto emphasizes shikantaza. The "participant mode" encourages a pseudo-Rinzai approach, confusing excitement and emotional upheaval with the ardor and drive required by the Rinzai way. But beyond these two modes is the witness—pure presence, pure awareness. Witness is a ringing stillness, a living silence out of which everything emerges, including not only sound but all color, shape, smell, sensations, activity and inactivity, and motion and the motionless.

When the mind is quiet, stillness can be heard. Even in the midst of a disaster or in a battle, stillness is present. The witness—clear, pure awareness—is never absent. Nisargadatta says, "When the mind is quiet, we withdraw from the experience and its experiencer and stand in pure awareness." The expression "the experience and the experiencer" is another way of talking about the participant and the observer. This withdrawal is already a great step forward in the practice. However, you must be careful because just seeing into the stillness is not the end of practice by any means. Bassui, in *The Three Pillars of Zen,* warns us against stopping when we encounter this stillness and quiet. He says, "With the passage of time one's thoughts are stilled, and one experiences a void like that of a cloudless sky. You must not, however, confuse this with awakening." He says we must go on, go deeper. "Only after your search has permeated every pore and fibre of your being will the empty space suddenly break asunder and your face before your parents were born appears."

The error we often make is confusing either the observer or the participant with the witness. This leads us into a rigid inner life on one hand, or a very chaotic inner life on the other. The painter is part of the painting; the experiencer is part of the experience. Your reaction to the situation is part of the situation. Both observer and participant are the witness. People say, "I'm really fed up; I just don't know what to do. I'm so tired, I'm so sick of everything; I really wish I knew what I could do." Now the "I" that is so tired, that is so sick, that so wishes it knew . . . is also part of the situation. All of those feelings exist within a medium; the medium is the stillness, and beyond the stillness is the "face before your parents were born," "the sound of one hand clapping." We cannot sort things out at the level of the experiencer and the experience, the level of the participant and the observer. All that is possible at this level is either a truce or war. Peace is beyond them both. In meditation we should not seek peace, because such a search would be carried on at the level of the opposites, using one kind of strategy or another, and this at best gives a temporary resolution. We must go *through,* not *out of,* the situation.

The personality is based on self-identification as "I" imagines itself to be *something* and says, "I am this" or "I am that." Self-identification comes out of the need to gain a focus or orientation point, which in turn comes out of a basic need of life—to situate ourselves. In the past human beings have used many different ways of ensuring an orientation point or center, and I deal with this at some considerable length in my other books. Originally the point of focus was "outside": a sacred tree, a totem pole, a flag, a rock, an idol, each of these has in the past served as a center, a basic orientation point around which to structure what we know as experience and existence. Nowadays we have introjected the center and call it "I." However, "I" is a promise; it is something that we are going to attain. We are constantly on the run after the possibility that at last I'm going to find out what I am. This is the cause of much of our exhaustion and despair. Just letting go makes us feel very uncomfortable, because letting go is not letting go into peace but into the very conflicts and uncertainties that give rise to our need to find out who or what we are. But if we let go in this way, we can pass through these machinations, this clashing and clanging of the personality.

The feeling that we may have—that we are soon going to reach a final goal, achieve final and absolute stability and security—keeps the wheel of pain turning. We push ourselves to reach some final destination, be it a relationship, a position in a company, some recognition, and so on. This pushing is not always in a positive way either. People can push themselves in a negative way, turning in more and more upon their pain and sadness, hoping in this way to find final security, feeling that if only they could be just a little bit more miserable, they would really find out what it is that they are. Hurting oneself in this way also comes from the same need to identify, to find out finally what one is.

Some, probably most, people fear that if they really were to wake up; if they really were to push the question "Who am I?" through to a conclusion, they would at that moment cease to exist altogether. This fear—that I would somehow disappear—haunted my early practice. I was afraid that awakening would not be a fulfillment but an engulfment. It is difficult to describe, but the feeling was one of being at the crumbling edge of an abyss. This fear dogged me with horror for a long time. However, it is not awakening that is the problem but identification, which carries with it the belief that one is, or at least should be, absolute. The world persistently refuses to accept our claim, and so we become an ambitious, pushy, forceful, ever going on kind of person. We feel, "I've just got to do a little bit more and I'll make it absolute." This feeling is what snaps. The belief that we can achieve ultimate consummation by being something in the world gives way. Everything else goes on as always, but instead of being self-motivated dynamic engines we become like puppets. Before this can happen we have to face up to and let go of the need to be absolute and, at the same time, distinct individuals.

You may well ask, "What is the point of this, what is the point of knowing yourself? What good does it do? What good will it do me if I do know this?" This question comes from a modern, but very strange, idea that everything must serve some purpose, everything must have a use; that nothing has an end in itself. This attitude is what causes stress and makes us harried in life. While we hold to this idea, we cannot just sit down and read a book, enjoy a conversation with someone, or even enjoy a good meal, because what we do has to serve a purpose; it has to have meaning. As we practice, so it becomes evident that everything has its own meaning. It is not necessary for anything to serve anything else because everything is intrinsically valuable. Yasutani Roshi used to say that even a cracked cup is perfect. In whatever way you are, even if you are a cracked cup, you are still perfect, you don't have to serve anything else, you don't have to be a useful person in the world. By this I do not mean that you do not have to fulfill whatever obligations life happens to have brought you. Of course, you should fulfill these obligations and fulfill them as well as possible, but you should let go of the claim that anything you do has an ultimate, absolute value.

Philip Kapleau in a talk that he once gave, told us about a man who was a doctor, who had been through the Pacific war and had experienced some of the horrors of that war. These experiences shattered his whole sense of equilibrium. After the war he was tormented by depression and anxiety so much that he did not know what to do. Constantly he asked himself, "What am I here for? What use do I have? What must I do?" Because he was a doctor he also asked himself, "What is the point of being a doctor? What good does it do?" He allowed himself to be completely taken over with this question, or perhaps it was not so much that he allowed himself as he just could not help but be overtaken by it. Eventually, however, he broke out of his depression. He said to himself, "I'm a doctor because I'm a doctor. That is enough!" Whatever you're doing, whatever role in life that you have, do it but without any wish that it should be useful. It is not necessary to have the feeling that you are serving some ultimate destiny of the world. This need arises when we are searching for an identity and want this identity to be absolute and therefore exalted. When we can let this kind of game go and just come home to ourselves, then we find, as Zen master Hakuin says, "This earth where we stand is the Pure Lotus Land. This very body the body of Buddha."

Truth, goodness, harmony, and beauty manifest spontaneously, but most people are not aware of this. Our conflicting desires, our attitudes, our wanting to grasp and grab, our wanting to *be* and be superior, and all the rest of it inhibit this awareness. But when things are left to themselves, not interfered with, not shunned or wanted, not conceptualized but just experienced, then full awareness shines through. Just allow whatever is there, whether it's beautiful or ugly, good or bad, something evil or something blessed. Just stay with it. Such awareness is pure knowing, which does not make use of things and people but fulfills them.

Trust your deepest intuitions! You are not alone!
You are not mad! You are not losing your way!
You are on your Way!

—Angelus Silesus

CHAPTER ELEVEN

Lighting a Fire

Zen practice is something like this. Suppose you are out camping and want to light a fire for warmth and to cook by. You have just one match, and it rained just a while ago and the ground is still damp. What do you do?

First, you light a few leaves, dry ones. Then you gather a few more and gently add them to the flame. Then a few more. Perhaps now a twig or two and more leaves. More twigs now and a few small branches. Careful! A few more smaller branches can be added to what is now a small blaze. Now some bigger branches. Not too big! Now some more, and more. Now those bigger branches. Soon a roaring fire throws its heat and light around the camp. If you want to, you can now put whole trees on the fire, even burn down the forest itself.

why does it rain
    on the sea?

Wonder of Wonders

Zen practice is not simply sitting on a cushion in a zendo, facing the wall, following the breath, or working with a koan. The heart of Zen practice—and indeed of all spiritual practice—is perplexity, wonder, care, concern, in the face of our human situation. We only have to pick up a newspaper to realize how true are Shakespeare's words: "What a tangled web these mortals weave." How contradictory are our lives; how full of pettiness and greatness, stupidity, and wisdom. In the same newspaper we read that a rocket is about to circle Jupiter and also that scientists have been pouring atomic waste into rivers. During the Falklands War a story was told about a young Argentine pilot who made a courageous attack on the British fleet, homing in on a destroyer, seeking to sink it with an Exocet missile. He was shot down, but no sooner was his plane in the sea than seamen from the very destroyer that had been under his attack and that had shot him down were risking their lives rescuing him; then the ship's surgeons battled to save his life. In the Vietnam War whole villages were destroyed in order to save them. Indeed, what a tangled web we mortals weave.

In our own lives the same contradictions abound: we can love and hate someone at the same time; we are forever making unreasonable demands on the world, but still our hearts are full of tenderness and gentleness. As St. Paul said, "That which I would not, that I do; that which I would, that I do not." Yet, it is not simply our contradictions that make us wonder. Consider all the different ways people live or have lived, all the different societies and civilizations that have come and gone: the Australian Aborigine living off the desert, the cowboys in the Old West, the Eskimos making their homes in the inhospitable waste of the Arctic, the Aztecs with their massive human sacrifices, the crowded cities of the industrial world, all of the widely different but totally self-contained ways that human beings have lived. Then consider the remarkable things that individuals do: skaters whirling round three or four times in the air, high divers plunging hundreds of feet, skiers racing down steep slopes, swimmers swimming under the sea, hang gliders, astronauts, mountain climbers. Think of the complexity of mathematics; the intricacy of theoretical physics; the fecundity of music; the artistry in Rome, Florence, Venice, Paris; the paintings, carvings, architecture. And then think of the advances in medicine, electronics, space travel. Think of airplanes routinely taking off with hundreds of people aboard. When we meditate on all this and then remember how millions upon millions upon millions of people live, work, love, and laugh together, and all against the background of suffering, pain, anxiety, sickness, accident, old age, and death, we just have to wonder. To ask what is it all about doesn't touch it. Such a question is banal in the face of this fountain of miracles.

Even so, in spite of this banality, we cannot help asking, "What does it all mean, what is it all about?" because these words come out of our bewilderment. When we practice a spiritual way, we let go more and more of the things that are obstructing the arousal of wonder and open ourselves to this marvelous mystery of being, which is still just one dust mote in the great universe of life.

Wonder basically is nonseparation. It is seeing what is so unseeable, so ungraspable that, at a deeper level, we cease trying to grasp it; when we do so, then we are one with it; this is faith. A Christian mystic said, "If faith, then faith." If faith is needed, then only faith is required. If we could penetrate this saying, we would go right through to the bottom of all the confusion. If faith, what need of results? What need of changing things, getting things, getting rid of things? If faith, then faith. But so often we use faith as a bribe. We say to God, "I'll have faith in you, but you must deliver." And when he doesn't deliver, we complain, saying, "I had faith in him, so why is all this happening to me? Was my faith not strong enough?" Acting like this is acting like a merchant trafficking in magical results for which he is prepared to pay with what he calls faith. If we pray to God and the prayer comes out of faith, then nothing else matters. Whatever we do for the sake of truth takes us to the truth, because it comes out of the truth. *Faith* and *truth* are words describing our true nature. Faith is that knowing which supports everything. Everything that for us is, is known, is supported by knowing. What we hear, see, touch, taste, smell, all comes out of knowing. And this pure, unconditioned knowing is what we call faith.

Everything that we do—whatever it may be, no matter how perverted or strange it might seem to others—comes out of faith and is, in its own way, a search for our own self; everything that we do is religiously motivated, if one looks at religion as the search for wholeness, for the holy, for oneness. The problem, however, is that so much of what we do is misguided; so instead of bringing us the unity and harmony we seek, it simply aggravates the situation, making us more divided in ourselves, more separated from others. And so we are forced to act again, often in a precipitous manner, which again makes matters worse, and so on.

One of the reasons we sit in zazen is that it helps curb the restlessness that otherwise overtakes us. Anyone who has wondered in the way I suggest knows how restless, how irritable at some level, we become. We just cannot stay with it. Sitting in zazen, with a straight back and low center of gravity, little by little, we open ourselves to the energy that wonder releases in us. The same restlessness comes with the urge to create and when we practice Zen in the midst of wonder; we are artists without art: we sit with this urge to create, this creative hunger, without giving it a form upon which to rest. Sometimes instead of creative hunger we may feel love. We may even love someone specific; at other times we may just love, like a light shining. But unless we are well anchored and have disciplined ourselves in not allowing images, ideas, and thoughts to chew up this energy; then we are unable to open ourselves to any degree. With a straight back we can let go of the concern about the body. With this and a low center of gravity, we can reach a state wherein our attention is totally free.

We can easily get carried away by the exotica of a spiritual practice. The Zen Buddhist tradition, for example, has great beauty, particularly for the Westerner who encounters it for the first time. It is like a drink of cool water on a hot day. What the Zen masters say has an austerity, a clarity; the meditation room has the sheer beauty of simplicity; the monk's robes and bald head have an appeal; the posture has great dignity; the chanting, a power—and it is so easy for us to get swept up by the exotica, the trappings.

However, we must pass on swiftly beyond the exotic; we are not engaged in a mystical activity in which we try to encourage a mystical state of mind above and away from the clash and clang of everyday life. Zen practice is not something that we do now and again: Zen practice and life are not different. Work is in progress in the universe, and we are participating in that work. We are not trying to flee from reality; reality is the substance of our practice. This is why so often practice presents itself in terms of pain and anguish, even deadness and inertia. Furthermore, we are not working for the personality. Somebody who has really worked doesn't know how to answer another who asks, "What are you doing it for?" One is puzzled by this kind of question. Why does the sun shine? As long as we see ourselves as isolated and separate, something either apart from the world or in the world, the question "What am I doing it for?" can arise. The truth is that the world and I are one; the world and all that can arise in or outside of the world, all heavens, and all hells, are not separate from what I could call "me." Practice is realizing this; and so, as this spells the end of all conflict, why wouldn't we want to realize it? But truth cannot be expressed in words, however hard we try.

On the other hand, we must be careful with the tendency found among Zen groups to put down words. Words cannot convey reality, but nevertheless it is because of words that we can realize this is so. Of all contradictions, language is probably the greatest. By language we don't mean just the spoken word, but all kinds of language: music, painting, dance, mathematics—all of them in their own way release us. But all language in its own way also binds us.

As Nisargadatta says on one occasion, "Only be earnest and honest. The shape practice takes hardly matters." If we are earnest, we are very careful to ensure that our practice is not a fidget, that it is not doing something for the sake of doing something, doing something to get rid of the tortuous sense of lack, of missing the boat, of missing something essential in life. But on the other hand, if we are earnest, then we realize how difficult it is to be earnest—just as if we are honest, we know that honesty is almost impossible. People often ask, "What is the point of my trying to practice? I can't keep my mind still for two minutes." A question like this comes from a lack of earnestness. St. Paul is quoted earlier as saying, "That which I would not, that I do; that which I would, that I do not." He did not say, "So what is the point of it all?" What he said was an expression of his earnestness, his honesty. When we have seen how the mind flits and flutters, comes and goes, is full of all kinds of extraneous, unnecessary, greedy, lustful, angry thoughts and yet nevertheless we continue—this is earnestness and honesty.

One could say that even mere greed or desire or lust undiluted by thought and action—pure concentrated greed— may be fuel to the practice. But the problem is greed, desire, and lust invariably come out of conflict and separation and are so often inextricably intermingled with thought and image. However, if they are accompanied by a longing, a yearning without any formulation of what we are yearning for, then even these emotions eventually become unified, transmuted into energy, and so fuel the longing even more. Christ said, "Blessed are they that hunger and thirst after righteousness." Just to be with the hunger and thirst, earnestly, honesty—that is practice.

But often we do not have the luxury of rage or lust or greed to fuel our practice; instead, we are faced with endless, dull repetition, boredom, and dry despair. How can this have any value? How often have we asked this during our practice, when we are mechanically struggling with a koan, the koan no longer in our minds, and we are no longer even sure what the koan is supposed to be or what we are supposed to be doing with it? How we are supposed to work when the practice has almost come to a stop, and we are lost in a lunar landscape, hot and dry? How can this be of any value whatsoever?

We try to judge practice in the way we have always judged things, by whether it makes us feel good; whether it gives satisfaction, pleasure, comfort, happiness; by what it does to sustain the personality, what we like to call "enriching the personality," but is so often simply making it bloated and inflated. But we cannot judge spiritual practice in this way. Most people under these circumstances just give up. But if they have been bitten by the bug of wonder, by the need to know in a way that the world cannot know, cannot teach, then they can never give up.

Some people come to awakening at their first sesshin. Some people who come to awakening never even go to a sesshin. Others practice for years and years and years. It does not matter. In the same way that we can't judge the success of a Zen Center by the number of its members, so we cannot assess another in terms of speed of awakening. To have committed ourselves is already success; the rest doesn't matter. When we have said yes deeply, nothing beyond matters. Even if for a while we stop practicing Zen, it does not matter because sooner or later we shall start again or take up another discipline. Until then something will nag at us; we shall have a feeling of the inappropriateness of everything else we do; we shall feel like we are wasting time. To have said yes is like a seed having germinated; a foot-thick layer of asphalt may be covered over it, but even so it will push its way through.

But this push does not come from self-will. This is why practice done in spite of the protest of the ego is the real practice. Many people, particularly when they first start, are all abuzz. In the sixties, when I first started my own practice, some of the other members would sit all day and all night. I used to think, "My goodness, these people are really working hard. I don't know how I could ever do anything like that." But if you looked closely, you could have seen that as these people sat in meditation, they would look out of the corner of their eye to see if some other person were still meditating. If he or she was not, then they would start getting restless and would soon leave the zendo. But if that other person were still there, then they would get back to it again, back straight, eyes down, puffing and blowing. This was self-will, a contest: who was going to do the most, the longest, the hardest, zazen.

This kind of practice cannot be sustained. The will that comes from desperation or after we have been thoroughly disappointed by everything but nevertheless refuse to roll over and die is the will that will carry us through all blocks and barriers on the Way. This is why Zen master Hakuin says that practice carried on in the midst of the fire is a hundred thousand times more valuable than practice on the cushions and mat. If in moments of deep despair that come in life, when we do not know what to do next, we go and sit—then this is the real practice. Nisargadatta says, "Spiritual practice is will asserted and reasserted. Who has not the daring will not accept the real even when offered. Unwillingness born out of fear is the only obstacle." The real is always black, dark, unknowing, and unforgiving because awakening to the real is the death of ego. Without earnestness and honesty, we can never pass through this death.

—·—·—·—·—·—·—·—·—·—·—·—·—·—·—·—·—

> *Man has to awaken to wonder; science is a way of*
> *sending him off to sleep again.*

—·—·—·—·—·—·—·—·—·—·—·—·—·—·—·—·—

—Ludwig Wittgenstein

CHAPTER THIRTEEN

A Glass of Water

"All that we are is founded on our thoughts, it is made out of our thoughts."

—Dharmapadda

Two figures trudged through the heat and dust. At first black shadows, they emerged from the glare and shimmer of the sun—an old man, bent, weary; a young man, alert, solicitous. They came to a tree throwing its shade aslant the track; some twenty feet beyond the tree lay a small cottage slumbering on the banks of a dried-out river. The old man sat wearily in the shade. He asked, "Elam, will you please bring me some water from that cottage?"

"Yes, yes, I'll be right back," replied Elam.

The young man turned quickly, went to the house and knocked on the door. After a few moments a young girl of striking beauty opened the door. She smiled gently and asked somewhat shyly, "Good day. Can I help you?"

"My teacher is weary and thirsty. Could you please give me some water for him?"

"Of course. Will you not come in for a moment while I get it for you?" Elam walked in and, at the girl's invitation, sat down. "Could I get you a drink as well?" she asked.

Elam agreed, and when she brought him the drink, they talked and found to their surprise that they were both born in the same small town some ten miles away. They searched their memories for some common experiences, friends shared, places visited, and soon found that they had much in common. Lana, for that was the girl's name, insisted that she get something for the young man to eat. Gradually the afternoon merged with evening, and evening with the dark of night. Elam realized that he could no longer live without Lana, and Lana in turn looked down and smiled.

One thing led to another, as is so often the case in these kinds of things, and they declared their love for each other, became betrothed, and eventually married.

During the rainy season the dried-out river became a fast-moving waterway, and by hard work and by using different kinds of irrigation devices, Elam managed to develop a large area of the land as a garden for growing many different kinds of fruits and vegetables. Lana too helped from early morning to late in the evening. They did so well that they were able to supply a good deal of the neighboring villages with fruit and vegetables.

In time, they had two babies. First, a girl was born and then, just over a year later, a baby boy. Elam with the help of some neighbors enlarged the house and made a beautiful garden full of flowers in which the children could play under the watchful eye of Lana.

Their lives prospered, and as the years passed, their love grew ever deeper; they felt sure nothing could ever mar their joy. However, one year the rainy season was much more severe. It started earlier and rained hard until soon it poured down in sheets. The wind blew great gray clouds, lightning flashed and flickered, and thunder rumbled. Day after day it rained, heavier and heavier, until earth and sky became a single wash of water. The river rose up its banks and flooded over the hard-won garden, which became first a marsh, then a lake. But still it rained. The waters inched up the walls of the house. Elam moved his small family to the second floor.

At first he had not worried very much. The rainy season was always a very wet one. The more rain, the easier it would be to irrigate the land. But now it had rained too long, the waters were rising too fast, and who knew whether the dam that caused the river to dry out each summer would hold. He sat and looked anxiously at the river, hour after hour, day after day, peering through the streaming rain, trying to judge from the movement of the water whether the dam was still holding. All through the night he sat while Lana slept peacefully and trustingly by his side, cradling the young baby in her arms, her daughter lying but a few short feet away.

Dawn came. The black of night gave way to a gray sullen streaming day. As he looked, his eyes worn and sore, a wave rolled down the river, and another, then another, bigger one. The dam had burst. "Quickly! quickly!" he cried, "We must get out." But even as the family struggled out of the drug of sleep and got ready to go down the stairs, Elam saw that it was already too late. The water rose steadily and swiftly up the side of the house. The first floor was already lost to the water, which was now greedily lapping its way into the second story. He cried out to Lana, "We must get out onto the roof! Any minute now it will be too deep in here for the children."

First, Lana forced her way through the narrow window that opened onto the sloping roof, and then Elam passed the two frightened children out to her. Already knee-deep in water, he followed his small brood out onto the roof, exposed to the biting, rushing wind and pelted by rain. They clung to the peak of the roof, shivering, looking across the vast landscape, a water wasteland of terror.

The wind tugged and pulled. Lana clung desperately to her children, trying to anchor herself so that she would not slip down the steep slope of the roof. Elam clung to her. All around was nothing but water and debris carried by the water: dead cows and struggling horses, trees, roofs of houses, carts—all bobbed and jostled their way down the center of this gray, freezing torrent.

Lana turned to Elam. "I'm getting so tired. Will you not hold the baby for a short while to give me a chance to rest?" She reached out to pass the baby boy into the outstretched arms of her husband but, as she did so, struck the little girl, who lost her hold and began to slip down the roof. Lana cried out in anguish and stretched down to catch the little girl and just caught her dress. But then she too began to slip, and the only way to stop herself would be to let go of the girl—and this she would not do. Faster and faster both slid, and Elam put the boy down and managed to put his foot far enough down the roof for his wife to grab it and check her fall. Husband, wife, and daughter were strung out on the wet, slippery roof suspended in a time of agony. The baby boy cried, rolled over, and slid down the roof. The father lunged out, dislodging his wife, and she plunged down, following her two children into the swirling waters to be swept along with the rushing flood bearing its strange and demented cargo.

Elam clung to the roof. First, he saw a small hand, then his wife's face, then a foot, and then all was gone. The rain lashed down, the water mingling with his tears of grief. The wind blew and moaned, and deep in the depths he heard his teacher say, "Won't you please knock on the door again? I am very thirsty and would like a drink." Elam turned and knocked again, but he knew the house was empty.

— · — · — · — · — · — · — · — · — · — · — · — · — · —

The master asked, "Where were you this summer?"
The monk replied, "I'll tell you when you have a place
to stay."

— · — · — · — · — · — · — · — · — · — · — · — · — · —

On Pain

Pain inflicted upon us by others is far different than pain arising from situations of our own choosing. Many sports require considerable pain and effort when training. Olympic-class divers practice at the Complexe Claude Robillard swimming pool, a site of the 1976 Olympics and quite near the Montreal Zen Center. They do many different kinds of dives that are very demanding: somersaults and backflips, spins and twists. Often they hit the water awkwardly. The shock and pain that comes from such a crash must be considerable. During practice they get no recognition, no applause, no inducement to continue, and yet up they go again, up to the top diving board, and off they fly once more. Time after time, hour after hour, these people put themselves through it. So it is with anyone who does this kind of Olympic training: running, jumping, and gymnastics all demand constant effort, all demand that one returns again and again to work after, even in the midst of, pain.

But this kind of pain is quite different from what you feel when, for example, a bully deliberately hits you. This pain can be intolerable even though, physically, it may be much less severe than what comes during training. It is not the pain itself but the circumstances surrounding the pain that determines whether it is tolerable.

Whether something is pleasant or unpleasant, pleasurable or painful, lies ultimately in whether one can accept it: actually accept it. Although it may seem a small point, perhaps it would be better if we were to use the expression "to be one with" rather than "accept." This modification in wording may seem just a question of semantics, but it is not really so. When we *accept* something, it is often because we have no alternative. It is often a case of "I don't like it but I suppose I just have to accept it; I just have to put up with it, don't I?" This kind of acceptance is at the basis of some Stoic philosophy. The Stoic philosopher says that life is suffering, but one has to accept the suffering in life—one has to put up with it. This attitude underlies many people's reaction to suffering: "I can do nothing about it; therefore, I have no alternative but to accept it."

However, something much more basic than mere acceptance ("I have to put up with it") is implied in "being one with" the pain. The Christian counterpart to "being one with" is found in the Lord's Prayer: Thy will be done. We have suggested this line as a mantra, and later as a koan, for practicing Christians who nevertheless wish to benefit from Zen practice. "Thy will be done" is one of those bottomless statements. On the face of it, it looks as though one is saying, "Well, I accept thy will; I accept what is happening." But when you penetrate it more and more deeply, one realizes ultimately that "Thy will be done" and "being at one with" whatever happens are not different. A bird singing, the leaves rustling as the wind blows, the rain falling, your legs hurting as you sit for long hours in meditation, are all God's will being done as long as you are one with them. If you are one with the devil, you can be happy in hell. If you are at odds with the angels, even heaven will be painful. Suffering, on the other hand, comes from the unwillingness or, one might say, the inability to be at one with the situation.

Some time ago a father and a son wanted to come to a seven-day sesshin at the Montreal Zen Center. At first I refused to accept their application because, as the application was being made by phone and I had not met them in person, I did not know them sufficiently well to judge whether they would be able to undertake a long sesshin. I said, "I think you will have to come for a shorter period, for a four-day sesshin." They protested a great deal, saying that they had been practicing meditation for a long while, that seven days would present no problem to them, and so on. However, I insisted and said, "You must come for four days of the retreat only, and in any case when you come, you must sit for one day and then, at the end of that first day, come to dokusan [individual instruction] to commit yourself to how long you will stay, but this must not be for more than four days." "Oh," they said, "all of this is so unnecessary."

Anyway, they came. I saw them before the sesshin started and again said to them, "You must be able to commit yourself to this kind of sesshin, because it can create problems for you in the future and is not good for other people attending the sesshin if you just break away and leave. So, wait until you have done one day and then make up your mind." "Oh, we won't break away."

The first dokusan arrived. First of all, the son came in; he was in tears. "I don't know that I can go on at all," he said. "This is too much." So, we spent some time talking together, and eventually he said, "I'd like to do a two-day sesshin." "OK," I said. "You're going to do a two-day sesshin." Then the father came in and nearly bit my head off. He was shouting at me, "This is ridiculous! What you are doing to these people is brutal. I don't understand what your attitude is or what you are doing. I am not staying for another minute!"

So, sure enough, off they went. In fact, they went off in such a hurry that they forgot half their belongings.

Now, here were two people (the man was in his late forties, I suppose, the son in his early twenties) who were simply unable to tolerate the pain, even for one day. They felt that this pain was beyond anything they could bear. Furthermore, and this is important, they blamed me and the way the retreat was being run. It was, they felt, the situation—not themselves—that was at fault. They seemed to feel something malicious was being done and that I was acting in a malicious way toward people.

This is not meant as a criticism of these two people. What it shows is that they had separated themselves from the pain. Others, some much older, much more frail (one lady is seventy-eight; another, a monsignor of over seventy; another, an ex-college professor of seventy), come for retreat after retreat after retreat. The pain in the legs—the pain from the *kyosaku,* the hardship of having to rise early in the morning and to continue hour after hour—that the father and son suffered and what these others, who come back time and time again, suffer is not different in any real way. The men had no particular physical problems; on the contrary, they were quite fit. But they had a wrong attitude—an arrogant, brash attitude toward what was going on—and it was this that prevented them from being sufficiently open and able to be one with the pain. It was the resistance, the separation, that made the pain intolerable, *not the pain itself.* This, furthermore, is true not only of physical pain but of all kinds of pain, of all the suffering in life: physical, psychological, and moral.

During a sesshin one suffers different kinds of pain: the pain that comes from being told what to do, which entails its own kind of pain; the pain that comes from having to sleep in strange surroundings in the company of people you do not know too well; the pain of not being able to talk and of having to maintain silence, of having to keep the eyes down. In addition is the pain that comes from sitting long periods with its attendant pain of anxiety and rage, as well as the pain that comes from, well, we can call it dryness. This pain that comes from dryness, from the desert, from there being nothing at all that has any interest in the situation, could be looked upon as the worst pain of all. Many people, when faced with it, go into a panic. They simply can't face it. Indeed, it was almost certainly this that got to the father and son.

When totally one with the pain, we are going quite contrary to the whole habit patterns established not only by society but, you might say, by the biological system itself. By working with pain, by being open to pain, then like the carp, a symbol often found in the entrance to Zen monasteries, we are swimming against the stream of life and against the stream of what society accepts as normal. But because we are not relying upon simple instincts or habitual reactions that arise at the level of the personality, we must draw upon resources lying at a much deeper level, a level where the distinctions "me and this," "me and you," "me and them," "mine and yours," have not yet arisen.

During dokusan people who are experiencing a lot of pain sometimes say, "You know, if my wife [husband, friend, boss, or whoever] could see me doing this, they would laugh at me. They would think I was silly, stupid, doing this." But this means, for those who say it, that their pain comes not so much from the situation itself, as from being divided against themselves. He or she is seeing the situation, first of all, as it is, and then through the eyes of another. This Other may either be some particular person, such as a wife or husband, friend, or so on, or people in general, "they." If "they" could see me. . . . This other viewpoint always seems to be negative, cynical, ridiculing, bemused, and so very critical about what is going on. Being divided against oneself in this way happens not only in sesshins or when sitting in meditation but also in life generally. This means that when they come up against a situation in life, such people not only see it as it is but also see themselves in the situation through the eyes of another. Consequently, the pain is felt not only as itself but also as mirrored back from the other. This can cause the pain to build up until it becomes intolerable, much like feedback between a loudspeaker and a microphone.

Unfortunately, some of the teachings of the Church can exacerbate the problem. Many of us were taught when young that God could see whatever we did. The idea of an ever-watchful and critical eye was built into us by religion. Everything that we did would be seen through this ever-watchful eye of God. What this does, whether the ever-watchful eye is God's or a spouse's or a friend's, is to awaken, by giving form to, the deep schism that lies at the heart of our being,[1] a schism that divides us against ourselves and, by giving it form, holds it rigidly in place. Suffering, which is a constant background to life, is accentuated through constant feedback from the ever-watchful eye. We can let go of this feedback if we can see into it—that is to say, know it is there, recognize it for what it is, recognize the way it works. Then it is not necessary to struggle with it. We just let it go.

When you practice Zen, it is probably best at first (that means for the first ten years) not to tell too many people what you are doing. The fewer who know, the better. Most people will not understand because they will see what you are doing simply from outside, not from their own direct experience, and so naturally they see it as bizarre. The problem is that if you discuss it with them, you may well pick up this problem that we have just referred to, of seeing your practice through their eyes.

Our true nature *is* happiness (or perhaps *serenity* would be a better word to use). We know this: we know, at the deepest level of our being, that happiness is our right. St. Augustine says, "If you had not already found me, you would not be seeking me." If your true nature was not already happiness or serenity, you would not be seeking serenity. It is *because* this is so, because our true nature is serenity, that paradoxically we suffer, because we try to find happiness, peace, and serenity reflected in experience: in a love affair, in being famous, in owning many things, in having great wisdom, all of which are subject to the vicissitudes of life.

Why not go straight to the source? Why go in such a roundabout way, a way requiring that we have the approval of others, that we acquire a certain amount of belongings or knowledge or friends or foreign postage stamps or other kinds of "brownie points"? "That would be breaking the rules of the game," someone might say. It would be cheating to go straight to happiness without all the circumambulation, without putting up a target and getting others to accept it as the target, then getting others to help you reach the target, and then trying to beat all of them to the target (which somehow, in some way, seems to be the game). But even so, why not go straight to the source? Why not just work with happiness? Why not work with—or better still from—your true nature? Again, the paradox: to do so, we should have to give up our desire for happiness, bring to an end the self with its desires and fears, desires for happiness as well as fears that we shall not find it; and we are reluctant to do this, even though the self is the only obstruction to true happiness.

The only way to happiness is through Oneness: "to be at one with." The only way to peace is to let go of separation, of division, of the "it is all right over there but not so hot over here" feeling. This is what Zen practice is about, what following the breath is all about. People sometimes say to me, "Quite frankly, I don't really see what the connection is between my following the breath and my inability to really get into life. On the contrary, it seems to me that I am running away from life when I am sitting facing the wall, following the breath. I have got all kind of things going on—problems, fears, difficulties, antagonisms—and I just don't get the connection between coming to terms with all of that and following the breath."

A Zen teacher said that if you are one with a speck of dust, you are one with the whole world. To be "at one" is therefore not *quantitative*. If you are at one with an outbreath, at that moment you are at one with the whole world. The only way to know this is to experience it for yourself. To be completely at one with an outbreath is the same as being at one with pain. To be totally at one with pain, to look deeply into it, means that the separation between pain and pleasure breaks down. Both become experience, not *my* experience, *my* pleasure, *my* pain but just. . . .

Often when doing a spiritual practice, one comes face to face with the desert, a feeling of being abandoned, a feeling of dryness, and an endless sense of nothing to look forward to. At its most intense, it is not a feeling to which one can give a name. At first this is very painful, and one has a strong tendency to want to stir things up, to try to make something happen, to try this, do that. . . . But one has entered this desert because one has let go of the various ways one has used in the past to entertain oneself. These ways have, for the moment at least, come to an end. It is now possible for a much deeper unity to manifest itself, a unity that is not dependent upon an integration from outside. It is the entry into the state known in Christian meditative traditions as *apathea,* from which our word *apathy* has been derived but which means "freedom from feeling" rather than "absence of feeling." However, *apathea* most often first makes itself known in the desert.

If you encounter the desert, do not think that something has to be wrong with your practice or that you are not sufficiently "spiritual." As long as you feel something is wrong with the practice, you cannot bring your full awareness to what is going on at the moment. Instead, most of your awareness is given to finding some other way. This is why great faith is necessary—great faith not only in the teacher and the teaching but also faith in yourself; the faith that *you are capable of discerning the truth for yourself*. Ultimately, such faith is *already* truth and its discernment. It is also important to realize that although you may find some way by which to divert yourself for the time being and so escape this particular desert, sooner or later a desert will appear from which you can escape only if you are willing to spend your life skimming life's surface, scarcely living at all, living in a twilight zone in which ghosts encounter ghosts—a twilight zone wherein, alas, most people live.

Very often the dryness is accompanied by the inability to breathe freely. The breath is restricted and shallow, hot and harsh. Just be aware of the situation, be present to the restriction of the breath also. Don't try to breathe deeply, don't try to change the breath. Be present to the restriction of the breath. Sometimes the diaphragm is very tense—well, be present to that tension as well. Then, of course, hundreds of thoughts flit in and out like gnats on a summer's eve. Again, so there are thoughts. Recognize, without any kind of judgment, that these flitting thoughts have no connection whatsoever with one another or with the practice at the moment. If you do this quite dispassionately, you find that it is not necessary to bind them together, no need to take them into account or feel they have any importance at all, no need to claim them as "mine."

When we talk about being at one with pain, nonresistance, courage, and endurance, we are not talking about heroes or heroines. This deep courage and endurance is simply being one with your practice. If you get an image of being a hero, then, of course, the acceptance of pain becomes something quite different: you start to *inflict* the situation onto yourself. You make the situation into *something* over which you acquire a sense of power and superiority by being able to endure it. This is *not* what we are talking about, but just the opposite. If you feel any sense of puffing up, any sense of swelling, any sense of inflation that comes as a consequence of this kind of practice, then beware. It will lead to its own kind of terrible pain; and because it is, so to say, coming up from behind you, it is even more difficult to work with.

Just awareness: "here it is! here it is! this is what is present now!" And it is exactly the same way when one gets into high blissful states: one doesn't take off into the never-never. Always remember, *bliss that one can experience is not the bliss of one-mind.* Being present, not claiming the practice for one's own, not soaring away in blissful states, also takes courage, endurance, non-resistance: to be able to just breathe, in and out, not to make a big deal out of it, this is the practice. But this is bliss.

Sometimes people will ask, "Why should one deny one-self?" You can call what we are talking about a denial of the self, but it is not really so: one is not specifically denying anything. It is not that one is putting the self down, humiliating it, getting rid of it, or anything like that. To be "one with" is to be open to what is. The self, on the other hand, is to be closed to everything other than what "I" considers important. To be present to what is means to be present to what is unimportant as well as to what is important. This is what in Zen is meant by denying the self, and it is this that leads us into, and ultimately out of, the wilderness. Recognize right from the start that the practice holds nothing for the personality, that the personality gains nothing from it now or in the future.

> *Every living being longs always to be happy, untainted by sorrow;*
> *and everyone has the greatest love for him- or herself, which is solely*
> *due to the fact that happiness is his or her real nature. Hence, in*
> *order to realize that inherent and untainted happiness, which indeed*
> *one daily experiences when the mind is subdued in deep sleep, it is*
> *essential that one should know oneself.*
>
> —Ramana Maharshi

Chapter Fifteen

At Sea

O voyagers, O seamen,
You who come to port, and you whose bodies
Will suffer the trial and judgement of the sea,
Or whatever event, this is your real destination[1]

You are at sea. The boat you are in is small; it can scarcely carry one person with just a few provisions. The night is dark; no stars or moon relieve the gloom. You are lost. You do not know where land is, whether it is near or a thousand miles away. The wind is rising, gusting, and the waves get higher, white-crested, and—I forgot to mention—the boat has a leak. Not a really serious one, you can bail out the water, provided, that is, you keep on bailing. By turns you feel hopeful, then despairing, anxious, then cocky, afraid, then bold, panicky, then angry—angry at yourself for ever having gotten into the boat, at the guy who made the boat, at the stupid sea, at anything, anything and everything. You keep wishing things were different, that the boat were bigger, that it didn't leak, that you were near land. And then you forget to bail, the thing begins to founder, and in a sweat and fury you bail and bail until after a while things settle down. Or at least they're not quite as bad as they were.

It is cold and the wind gets stronger; now the waves wash over the side—not much, just a little now and again. But will it get worse, will you be able to bail enough? What will happen if, if, if? Thunder rumbles; you wonder What next? Can things get worse? You are so desperate, tears spring to your eyes. If only, if only. . . . Ceaselessly you search the darkness, but all you see is more darkness, opaque, impenetrable, menacing. What there is to see, what it is you are looking for, where to look for it, how to recognize it if you see it, you don't know. But you do know you must keep searching, searching, searching.

And then you see a light. It is definitely a light. There it is! It is a light. It is small; in fact, let's face it, it is so tiny and so far away, that it almost seems a mirage. But no, no doubt is possible, it is real. Relief washes over you. Just pure joy. A light means land. Not only is there really land, but it is right there and reachable. Not only is it reachable, but the light shows the precise direction to go. Mark you, your situation hasn't changed: the boat is still as small, it leaks just as much, the sea is still as rough, the night is just as dark. Indeed, in your moment of relief you've forgotten to bail and the boat is foundering! Quickly, get the bailer and start to work. But even so, the light shines.

Just keep going now, never mind about the fear and the hopes, the fear that there is no land, that you'll never find a direction, that it will be too far, that fate is against you. Even as all these fears rise up, they melt away in the reality of the light. The hope that when you see land it will be made of milk and honey, that you don't have to go to the land but simply have to wait for the land to come to you, that one day you'll wake up and find the sea has turned into land, that there'll be some wonderful reward for all the fears and labor, that you are the first, the best, the most intrepid of explorers—all these irrational fears and hopes, daydreams, speculations, and wishes rise up and melt away in the reality of the light.

If someone were to challenge you and say that it is not really a light that you are seeing, you would laugh and go on your way. Now you know the light that the sea threw up with its phosphorescence, that the imagination threw up in its terror and despair, that the intellect threw up in its futile attempt to regain mastery of the situation, all these were just phantoms,

phantoms of the past. The light is a sure beacon, and nothing can make you afraid of the dark and gloom again.

It's something like the words of the old Christian hymn:

Lead kindly light amid the encircling gloom,
Lead thou me on.
The night is dark and I am far from home
Lead thou me on.
I do not ask to see the distant scene
One step enough for me.

But still there is work. But as you work, you see yet another light and yet another; then a shape looms up, and another. These do not have the same impact that the first sighting of light had; they do not give the same utter relief from an intolerable burden of doubt and dismay, except perhaps when what you had thought to be a distant mountain turns out to be the roof of a warehouse not miles and miles away but almost within hailing distance. Each new light, each new shape, is but confirmation making deeper, more natural, and inevitable the original awakening. There is now a deep security in the awareness that you will reach land, that you will walk. Then even the possibility of foundering, and therefore the need to bail, will be no more.

But now you must work without haste and be fully committed to the work. You know that a certain distance must be covered, that a certain amount of water has to be bailed, that prayers, pleas, magic, or miracles will not take away the need for labor. Without dreams, these would just interfere. Without expectation, what is there to expect? Without hopes, these would be hopes for the wrong thing. One just goes on working.

But, of course, we have to be careful about all this. Analogies and metaphors can take us only so far and then they lead us astray because at best they can give us only half the story. We must be particularly careful of the metaphor of the light; many people have wandered around in never-never land because of this one. We even use the expression "He thinks he's seen the light" when we mean "He's completely deluded." Dogen tells the story of an emperor in the T'ang dynasty in

China who had a pagoda built in his palace. During the dedication service he suddenly saw a brilliant light shining in the hall. He was overjoyed by the vision and told everyone at court about it. All the courtiers except one congratulated him on his good fortune. The one who did not was a Buddhist. And the emperor asked him, "All the officials except you gave me congratulations. What is the reason for this?" The Buddhist replied, "Once I read in the sutras that the light of Buddha was not red, blue, yellow, white, or any natural color. The light that you saw was not the light of the Buddha, it was only the light of the dragon that protects you." Then the emperor asked him, "Well, what is the light of the Buddha?" The Buddhist remained silent.

We are not in a sinking boat; we are not at sea. We are not lost in the dark, and we cannot founder through lack of work. But let's face it, it sometimes feels awfully much as though we were. We don't need any guiding light either to light up the gloom or to lead us home. But we cannot help sometimes wishing it were there. A Zen master used to say, "The entire world is reflected by the eye of the monk, the entire world is contained in everyday conversation, the entire world is throughout your body, the entire world is your own divine light, the entire world is within your divine light, and the entire world is inseparable from yourself." This too is but half the story. It is as well to remember the story of a monk who was once asked, "Do you accept what your teacher tells you?" He replied, "I accept half of what he says." "Why don't you accept it all?" The monk said, "If I did, I would not be true to my teacher."

Although this is so, it is as well to be reminded about some of the things in practice. For example, it is as well to be reminded that it is not because we have made a mistake or that the teaching is wrong or that the teacher is off the wall that we find ourselves so far from land, even after we have practiced for a long while. Our practice has nothing for the personality; indeed, it is this very personality with its values and priorities, its likes and dislikes, expectations and demands, that separates us so completely from the source of life. In an age that has substituted personality for the soul, counseling for confession, and

junk food and beer before the altar of TV for the mass, to spend
time on something that has nothing for the personality is at best
sacrilegious, at worst, madness.

But true spirituality has never had anything for the personality. Christ said, for example, "Truly, truly I say to you,
unless a grain of wheat falls into the earth and dies, it remains
alone; but if it dies, it bears much fruit. He who loves his life
loses it, and he who hates his life in this world will keep it for
eternal life." This, like so much else in Christ's teaching, of
course has been misunderstood, because it can only really be
understood by someone who is a follower of the Way. Without
spiritual practice, all such statements are incomprehensible.
Such a saying as this does not mean that it is necessary to
undertake any special activity to "lose one's life," nor is it necessary to suppress one's love of life and develop instead cold, austere, puritanical behavior. It means that one does not sacrifice a
greater good for a lesser one, or as one Zen master put it, one
does not let the good stand in the way of the best. This is why it
is said that a Zen master will snatch a dry crust out of the hands
of the starving man.

It is also as well to be reminded that kensho, satori, awakening—call it what you will—both is and is not an *all or nothing*
affair. When at sea one sees the light; one sees it. At one
moment all is just darkness, the next moment there is light and
one's life is transformed. But there is still as much work to do as
ever. So it is with awakening. To wake up, to see for oneself that
"one" is whole and complete, to know the truth for oneself
without need of any intermediate thought or reason, that "one"
is beyond all form, that "one" is in truth the light of the world,
is sudden, and it transforms one's whole life. One will never be
the same. Awakening is the awakening of the intelligence; it is
Knowing, bodhi, or better still, Buddha. But there is still as
much work as ever to be done. Master Kuei-shan put it this
way:

> If one is truly awakened and has realized the fundamental, and
> is aware of it oneself, in such a case one is actually no longer
> tied to the poles of cultivation and noncultivation. But ordinarily,

even though the original mind has been awakened so that one is instantaneously enlightened in one's intelligence, there still remains the inertia of habit, formed since the beginning of time, which cannot be totally eliminated at a stroke. This person must be taught to cut off completely the stream of habitual ideas and views caused by the still operative karma.

There are several reasons why all this is emphasized. The first is that all of us have a certain amount of work to do, whether awakened or not. Some of us come to awakening and then do the work; others do the work and then come to awakening. Conscious work is never wasted. Another reason is to emphasize that most frequently the initial awakening is shallow. It is a "small light." This is why one must expect long practice on subsequent koans after the initial awakening. This practice brings other insights and new understandings all the time, but none of these has the same impact as the initial awakening.

Paradoxically enough, the fact that the initial awakening is a shallow one is good news for many. Such people may sometimes hold themselves back by the thought "I am not worthy of awakening," meaning by this that their lives and actions are so far from the wisdom, compassion, and peace they intuitively feel to be possible that they shy away from the very thought that they too can possibly come to awakening. Alternatively, others have the fear that awakening will so transform their personalities that they will be unrecognizable by others. But once we can accept that awakening can be of different depths, from very shallow to very profound, then we can see that there is a place for us all. As St. Thérèse said, "My father's house has many mansions with room for everyone."

Another reason for saying all this is that many people become discouraged when they see or hear about "people who are supposed to be awakened" acting in undesirable ways. Now and again one hears stories about people who are leading Zen Centers behaving in improper ways, and one wonders, What is the use of awakening if they can still act thus? I remember one person who said to me that he lost faith in the practice of Zen when he found that the legs of a particularly well-known Zen teacher were obviously cramped and stiff after a period of sitting. This is not to condone poor behavior; spiritual work most certainly does transform character, and in time much that passes for weakness is transmuted. But it is not done overnight, and much of the work is done from, so to say, the inside out and so may not be apparent for many years.

We must, therefore, keep both halves of the equation constantly in mind: one must practice as though one's hair is on fire. Dogen said that the practice calls for sweat, tears, and sometimes blood. On the other hand, as another Zen master said:

> To penetrate this kind of thing, you have to be this kind of person.
> Since you are this kind of person, why worry about penetrating this kind of thing?

The soul is constant only to this unknowing knowing which keeps her.

—anonymous

Fear of Failure

Is it possible to fail in practice?

Fear of failure can be a major obstacle for many people who are working on a koan. They are afraid that if they give themselves 100 percent to the practice, then perhaps they will be disappointed because they won't be able to make the grade. The result is that they tend to hold themselves back. A queer kind of logic supports this tendency: if I commit myself fully and fail, it will show that there is something wrong with me. Therefore, I won't commit myself fully. I know that I shall fail as a consequence, but it will not be because there is something wrong with me, it will be because I haven't committed myself.

But you cannot fail; when you commit yourself fully to the practice, this is of itself success. At one level it does not matter whether you practice or not, whether or not you take up Zen or any other kind of spiritual practice; you still cannot fail. Ultimately, you will come to awakening. Ultimately, the real, the true, must prevail. If you were not already awakened, you could never come to awakening. I often quote St. Augustine, who says, "If you had not already found me, you would not be seeking me." Your very presence here confirms that you are already awakened.

How do I commit myself? I don't know how to do this. What does it mean to commit myself fully?

Every night you give yourself over fully to sleep. Or when you go to the cinema, you give yourself fully to the film. It is true that a great difference exists between sleep and practice, but not in the commitment both demand. With sleep and when looking at a cinema show, awareness is clouded. With practice, awareness is not clouded. Nevertheless, you know how to commit yourself. And it is only fear that is holding you back.

Why does one practice?

One cannot help doing so. One cannot say the search that leads us to practice is "my choice"; it is not the personality that wants to practice. We practice because, being whole and complete, wholeness ceaselessly seeks to manifest itself. Every desire that we have ever had, or that anyone has ever had, is at bottom the desire for wholeness, for completeness. Happiness is to be "at one." Our constant search for happiness, the sense we have that it is our inalienable right to be happy, that somehow suffering should not be, comes from this fundamental wholeness that we already are.

But are there not many impediments to practice, particularly nowadays?

One of the things we recognize when we see into our true nature is that all we have passed through has been necessary. In Zen it is said, "One must exhaust the resources of one's being." "Exhausting the resources of one's being" is the journey. Many people like you ask whether the way they live is not an interference with their practice, whether those who can give up work, their families, doing things in the world, are not better off. And they wonder, because they have so many concerns and worries, whether they can find both the time and the energy to come to awakening. And yet, where we are is where we have to be. Where we are comes from what we are. And what we are comes from what we think, from our ideas.

When it is said that we must exhaust all the resources of our being, it means we have to fulfill these ideas. We have to live them to the fullest, and then go beyond them. It is not a question of giving up anything but of being ready to let things give us up. It is like when you were a child and had toys. The time came to let the toys go. It was not that you had to give them up; it was that they no longer fitted the bill, they were no longer appropriate and so they dropped away.

This is how to exhaust all the resources of your being. Whatever you do, do fully. And then when you have done it, be prepared to let it go or be prepared to let it let you go. This, of course, requires both honesty and courage; we so often confuse habit with need.

But aren't there some people who are not constantly blocked?

Everyone is addicted to something or other. Some are addicted to sex, others to success, others to knowledge, others to being a good person—some are even addicted to suffering. These addictions are obstacles, and working through them—seeing into their transitory nature—is not a waste of time. It has to be done. In Zen it is said that some people come to awakening and then they practice, others practice and then they come to awakening.

"To practice and then come to awakening" means that one works through these obstacles, these addictions, and then comes to awakening. "To come to awakening and then practice" means that one does exactly the same work. There is no difference. The advantage of the awakening is that now we work in the light; but the work is the same. But, when we see that we are indeed beyond form, then it is possible to use this openness as a way of dissolving the obstacles. Nevertheless, the work still has to be done.

I don't understand. Is not Zen supposed to be sudden? Are you not talking about a gradual practice?

One of the great problems of our age is the need for instant feedback, instant success. When Zen talks about sudden awakening, people confuse it with "instant" awakening. But instant success, like instant coffee, means no work precedes it. You do

ɔast the beans, grind them, percolate them, and all
hat goes into making the coffee; you just pour in
Most people want a practice where all they need do
ɔoonful of powder and pour in hot water. But sudden
g is not instant awakening. You have to grind the
beans.

But I get so depressed and often quite anxious about practice.

Your dissatisfaction, depression, and anxiety are valuable. They
come from a deep intuition of the truth that you have. When I
say you are whole and complete, you know. You don't even
need anyone to tell you this or bring it to your attention. You
know. You have always known, because your true nature is
knowing. Nothing is anterior to knowing, nothing comes
before it, nothing gives rise to it. Knowing is primordial. And
when I say you know, I do not mean you know something; I do
not mean, for example, that you know that you are whole and
complete, that you know you are awakened. I do not even
mean you know that you know. Knowing is enough.Wholeness,
completeness, awakening, *this is knowing*. Knowing, like the
light of day, is the atmosphere in which you live. It is ever present. It is not necessary for you to find something. Insofar as
there is this openness, this unobstructed quality, all obstructions are constantly giving way before it. But in that giving way
is a tension, dissatisfaction, anguish. This tension is, so to
speak, the interface between vast openness and the illusory
obstacle that is giving way, and comes from the wish to grasp
knowing in an experience, to experience unity as an experience.

*Sometimes when I listen to you I get the feeling you are saying that
the only purpose in life is to come to awakening.*

That is because you insist on making distinctions—in this case,
for example, between life and awakening. Life is the unfolding
of the awakened state. But we must be careful when we hear
this kind of thing, because people interpret it to mean that life
has no purpose. On the contrary, life is all purpose. Life and

purpose are the same thing. In other words, we don't have to find a meaning or purpose in life. We don't have to have some target in order to have a meaning and purpose in life. The reason that we feel life is without purpose, the reason that we get this sense of the not-going-anywhereness of life, is that first we have a target and then, for one reason or another, we lose sight of it. It has simply become obscured in the maze of the mind. When we let go of that target, we see that just in the same way that everything reflects light, so everything reflects purpose.

Why do we create targets?

We have targets when we ignore the truth that we know. Then, because we have targets, we have success and failure. Again, let me repeat that we do not have to stop doing what we are doing in life. What we are doing in life is what we have to do: it is not because we have decided to do it. When we decide to do something, we at last formulate in a conscious way what has to be done; before then we have a feeling of discontent. Therefore, it is only when we can formulate what has to be done that we can go ahead and do it. Indeed, the formulating and the doing are often coincidental.

But our problem is that we keep trying to decide in an *arbitrary* way what to do; we try to put into our lives arbitrary goals and purposes, and then success and failure enter because these arbitrary goals come into conflict with other goals, purposes, and ambitions that we create the following day.

When you sit, if you have a deep problem, sooner or later the very fact of sitting enables you to articulate what, until it is articulated, is a problem. Once it is articulated, it becomes naturally a part of your conscious experience. Working from the depths in this way—having a problem, sitting in the middle of a feeling of lack and need—is like koan practice. The difference is that with koan practice, it is not necessary to articulate the problem. You simply become it totally; you are simply one with it. Becoming one with this sense of problem, of dilemma, of need to resolve, of longing to express—just becoming totally one with it—is its resolution. In the end we must even let go of the very idea of becoming one with this. When we turn that need, that deep longing or yearning, into the need for some acquisition, some attainment, some new experience, we create the possibility of success and failure. In this way we can learn from failure.

What one can learn from failure?

When we fail, humiliation always follows. We feel shame. If we sit with that humiliation, we realize that we have tried something inappropriate. If it had been totally appropriate, we couldn't fail. And it is by re-experiencing these failures, these humiliations, that we are able to see the extent to which we are constantly doing what is inappropriate. A lot of the work that we do after awakening is working through shame and humiliation. We have to pay the price for everything that we have done. This is purgatory, the process of purging the soul.

The word *shame* in Tibetan is associated with the word *virtue,* and in Tibetan practice shame is one of the six virtues. Failure is the most direct route by which you can allow this virtue to manifest. To see this for yourself is a way of putting balm on the sting of failure. You can then commit yourself to the practice without any thought whatsoever of the outcome. You can then do it simply from the sheer love and life of doing.

Why do people who are awakened get involved in doing things? If you are awakened, why aren't you just completely impartial, dis-interested?

Quite the contrary! Now is the time that one *can* become involved. Now is the time that one can become totally interested. Totally interested, in a non-self-interested way.

What does that mean, in a non-self-interested way?

Seeing into the nature of failure, recognizing shame as a virtue, one sees that sadness and remorse are ways by which one comes home, by which one heals one's deepest wound. This means to say that one goes beyond self-concern, becomes non-self-interested. Again, one must always be careful how to interpret what is said. I am certainly not saying that one must wallow in unhappiness or that one must go out of one's way to be humiliated by life or to humiliate oneself. This is far from what I am trying to say. What we are talking about is that one can work with the natural ebb and flow of one's life. When one no longer tries to resist the ebb or to increase the flow, when one is able to work with depression, unhappiness, letdown, betrayal, and use it as a way to refine and clarify one's perception, then one no longer divides life into what is good and what is bad. This capability can only come out of practice. It cannot come out of a decision that one is going to undertake a certain way of life. It is not a question of listening to a talk and saying, "I'll do that, that, and that." When you are sitting and a different state of mind comes up, be with that state of mind. Let that state of mind be the state of mind to which you are present. Don't look for another. Don't look upon it as being inappropriate, wrong. Don't think, "I've got to get a move on. I've got to get to awakening. I've got to do this, I've got to do that." All these concerns are self-concern.

When you live in a non-self-interested way, you turn all failures into means for deepening practice and live in the light of knowing, what Christ called the light of the world. Nothing can darken or depress the light of day that you live in and that surrounds you constantly. Nothing can overwhelm or kill it. Just get a glimpse of this indomitable, fearless, ever victorious, being that is true nature. This is what we call kensho.

How then can we make use of difficulties in life?

When we reflect back on a time when we went through a great deal of difficulty, and analyze what was really difficult in that situation, we find a streak of pain cutting through the heart of the experience; it is almost like a geological fault. But this pain, when it first arose, transformed itself almost immediately into a series of thoughts and speculations. These in turn are very often fueled by the thoughts "What will happen if? . . ." "How bad can this get?" "It is all right now, but what about tomorrow?"

What will happen if? . . . If we could only extirpate those words, in some way, from our experience. We would still suffer pain. Pain is pain. But pain gives rise to imagination, and imagination then turns back and regenerates the pain, and a vicious circle is set up. The vicious circle can then start expanding until eventually we can get into a terrible panic. We feel that we just can't go on, things are really too much. But what is really too much are the thoughts that are inflating the thoughts. If we simply go back to the geological fault itself and sit with that pain and don't allow ourselves to latch onto this "What will happen if? . . ." then we find that the pain is just pure energy—but energy that is unable to find expression.

It is not the situation, it is what we make of the situation that gives us difficulty. Some people feel pain even when they are given good news—praise, for example. They have to turn it around into something negative. They can't accept it and are very uncomfortable.

Does awakening always have to be sudden?

Yes. If it is not sudden, it is not awakening. Practice is like paying off a mortgage: slow at the beginning and rapid at the end. It is slow at the beginning because most of the money you pay off is for the interest. But little by little, as you make payments, the principal is worn down. The time comes when most of your payment goes toward getting rid of the principal. In practice you will feel a deepening, an enriching of your life. And it is only then that you truly realize how wonderful the practice is. When you are paying off the interest, you are just learning how to stay there, how to be there. You struggle with thoughts and ideas, doubts about yourself, about the teaching and about the teacher. You keep wondering if there is not a better way, another way, or whether a way is necessary in any case. When you work with that and go on in spite of everything, that is paying off the interest. As you pay off the principal, a steady sense of immutability—something immovable—comes; a solidity begins to make itself known in the depths. But a moment comes when the mortgage is paid. It is like water boiling; suddenly it begins to bubble. It is like a crystal: for a long while the gel becomes more and more saturated. But suddenly, in a moment, the crystal appears.

But are we not all always awakened? Why all of this payment, this suffering?

At one level we are all always completely awakened. This is to say that everything that ever happens to us comes out of the intelligent source that we are. Each one of us is this total intelligence. Total intelligence mixed with experience gives what we call our life. Intelligence mixed with experience gives a feeling of progress, of acquiring, of attaining, of getting better, of becoming more capable. But we are simply circling; we are always coming back to the point where we started. When we get tired of this circling, when we are exhausted, for a moment we stop and question ourselves. And this questioning is a return, to some degree or another, to the source. Anyone who continues practice for any length of time has, to some degree or another, returned to the source.

Perhaps we are most vulnerable to this kind of return when we are young. Not so much in childhood, but in our youth. We have constant flashes that come from returning to the source, magic moments in life when we feel the spell, the magic of just being. As we move out of youth into adulthood, these flashes become more and more rare. Like Shelley said, "Rarely, rarely comest thou, spirit of delight." "Spirit of delight" is a wonderful way of talking about these moments of return.

Nevertheless, the perfume, the ambience, the feeling of total, clean freedom, lingers. Now and again, even in adulthood this burst of freedom, this spark, comes out. These moments of return to the source bring one to practice. So have faith in that. Have faith in yourself. You know. Even as you read this, a shadow goes across; you ask yourself, "What do I know?" "When he says I know, what do I know?" That is the shadow. We are not talking about "whats." The spark of freedom has no substance; it has no form; it is not a "what." It cuts through all "whats." It cuts through all forms. This is what makes it free.

Our practice is an invitation to return to the source. It is an invitation to allow the magic to come through the crack of uncertainty and doubt. When you stay with this question, when you give yourself over—in just the same way that you give yourself over to a film or a book or to someone you love—you make it possible for clarity to show itself.

Can we see this clarity then? If so, is it not something?

Although we speak in terms of returning to the source, and about sparks, the light of day, we must never forget that these are just ways of talking about our true nature. The light of day is not simply around us. It is us. It is our true nature. Everything that you know, that you experience, that you see, touch, smell, hear; every thought that you have; every feeling of anxiety or dryness, boredom, pleasure; every sensation and perception that you have, has as its basis and medium this light of day. Because of this no failure, no ultimate block, is possible. Everything, in its turn, will give way. When you sit—and you sit earnestly, honestly, simply—it is the direct route by which the light of day can be the light of your life.

_._._._._._._._._._._._._._._._._._._

> And when you pray, you must not be like the hyp-
> ocrites; for they love to stand and pray in the syna-
> gogues and at the street corners, that they be seen by
> men. Truly I say to you they have their reward. But
> when you pray, go into your room and shut the door
> and pray to your father who is in secret; and your
> father who sees in secret will reward you.

_._._._._._._._._._._._._._._._._._._

—Matthew 6:5

CHAPTER SEVENTEEN

The Donkey Who Would Not Work

A farmer had a donkey who would not work. The farmer did all that he could to get the donkey to work, but to no avail. Eventually, in despair he asked his neighbor for advice. "You must give the donkey lots of love and compassion," declared the neighbor. "Love and compassion!" exclaimed the farmer. "Yes," said the neighbor. "It works wonders."

The two separated, and the farmer returned to his donkey. After a couple of weeks the farmer happened to meet the neighbor. "How is the donkey?" asked the neighbor. "Is he working now?" "Not at all," said the farmer. "What you suggested has made no difference." "Let me see him," said the neighbor, and the two went off to find the donkey in a nearby stall. As the neighbor approached the donkey, he seized a two-by-four and, going straight up to the donkey, brought the two-by-four down onto the donkey's head with a sharp crack. "But," stammered the farmer, "I thought you said I must use love and compassion." "Yes," said the neighbor, "but first you must get its attention."

Purity of heart is to will one thing.

—Kierkegaard

145

CHAPTER EIGHTEEN

Fascination

Latin fascinere, fascinet: _to cast a spell on, from_ fascinum, _an evil spell._

We are not people or things among other people and other things in the "world." Our tendency to see "me," the "world," "others," and "things" as absolute, independent existences comes from an illusion caused by separation. It is useful to talk about "me" and the "world" the way we do in the same way a filing system is useful, but this view is conditional; it is relative. A filing system does not itself impinge in any way on the material that is filed. It does not alter the letters, correspondence, forms, or invoices in any way. But in life we have a tendency to make the system more important than the content. Our practice is a way of melting down this structure, of seeing into the conditional nature of the "world," "me," and "God."

The partitions, fences, and barriers of this structure are given by words. Words are wonderful creations. The original Word created the whole universe that we now know. One could say that there have been two creations: the creation of the world and the creation of the world as Word. But words are also binding and imprisoning; words are limiting. Nevertheless, when considering words we should dwell not only on their binding, limiting, and restrictive nature but also on their liberating, creative, and opening power as well. As long as we see words and thoughts only in a negative way, this itself will generate its own kind of separation.

One might well ask, "If I, the world, others, and God are illusions, how is it that I see the world? How is it that I was born and will surely die? You say that we are not separate individuals, that this separateness is provisional, illusory; so why is it that I am so certain I am a separate individual? Why do I feel that I am someone, something, somewhere?" These are good and necessary questions. It is in these very simple questions that the heart of spiritual practice resides. We must not be afraid to ask others and ourselves simple questions. We must not simply parrot others and repeat, "Everything comes out of words and thoughts," simply because people we respect have said such things. We must prove the truth of this for ourselves, test it for ourselves.

Whenever a good friend of mine gets the chance, she always asks me the most elaborate, philosophical questions. How does one deal with such questions? I want to respond, want to help her; but in the face of such questions, how? A snappy, Zenny response would be rudeness; but even so what she asks is so far removed from her or anyone else's experience that I cannot use my own experience to respond. To get help, we must ask simple questions. A story is told in Zen of the young monk who went to his teacher and said, "In the Prajnaparamita [a basic text chanted in many Zen monasteries and temples] it says, No eye, ear, nose, tongue, body, mind, but I have a nose, I have a tongue, I have a body. Why does it say that there is no eye, ear, nose, tongue, body, mind?" His question is a good one but easily overlooked. We are afraid to be innocent, afraid to be a neophyte, a beginner. We are afraid that people will think that we have not made much progress in our practice. But the real progress comes when we start looking at things as though for the first time.

Most people believe that they are the body. But why? We have a general kinesthetic sense—a general sensation of being that the body generates—and many people believe that this sensation of being the body is proof that this is what we are.

However, if we examine this a little more closely, we see that the feeling of being the body comes out of something much deeper. It comes from the feeling that *I must be something*. Logically, if I am not something, then I must be nothing; and if I really know that I am nothing, then I will fall into a pit of horror. Going from "I must be something" to "I am the body" is a very small step.

We are fascinated by this idea, "I am the body." Not only this idea, but life itself is fascinating. What do I mean by this? If we go see a film, we are most likely fascinated by it. We are "glued" to the screen. We enjoy being fascinated because it releases us in a certain way from a feeling of a binding irritation, a constant rubbing of two things against each other, of a friction in life. Anyone who has attended a Zen sesshin knows well what I mean by this feeling of binding irritation, particularly during an afternoon halfway through the sesshin. At this time fascination is far, far away; one is rarely fascinated by practice. On the other hand, our whole culture and civilization are about inducing fascination: books, plays, films, and, above all, television induce a kind of hypnotic state of being totally "swallowed up" by the situation. We are easily fascinated by both the beauty and terror of life. But by this we lose our sense of proportion, the sense of wholeness that is our true nature. We see the waves of the lake and forget the immensity of its depth.

It could be said that our practice is about reminding ourselves of this immensity. As we sit in zazen, every now and again we let go our grip on the surface and become aware of the mind's ability to operate at many levels. One has to be present to know what I mean because it requires great sensitivity and delicacy. It is more like a perfume than a vision. Being aware in this way gives a release also because one realizes that infinity is not an abstraction, that eternity is not simply a word, and that wholeness is not something among other things. Just a glimpse, a taste, is all one needs to rid one for the moment of the fears and frustrations, of the sense of life's being hopeless and pointless; to rid one of the pain of being alienated, of being on the outside of things. You know then that what you really are cannot be gauged, or plumbed, or estimated in any way.

148

Thoughts are just ripples in the mind. As one comes out of deep *samadhi,* one passes through this band of thought as ripples; at this level, when a thought comes, it is just like a pebble has been dropped into a lake: as the thought spreads out, so it stains the inconceivableness. Thoughts are stains. Seeing the staining quality of the thought "I," one sees its limitation. We are so taken in by this thought "I" that we think it is everywhere and everything. It is as if we were to put on rose-colored glasses—everything is colored rose red. Similarly, when we look through "I," everything is stained by "I." Our practice dissolves this stain by seeing that it has edges, limits.

We must not confuse Zen with mysticism, nor think of it as invoking heavenly, mystical, or magical forces. It does not. This is not to say that the very presence of "I" or "me" is not in itself a miracle, that seeing is not a form of magic. I am a miracle, seeing is magic, but there are no miracles outside the miracle of being. This is why it is said that everyday mind is the way. This is why also it is in the nature of things that we practice. We do not have to be a special kind of person to practice.

When the ripples in the mind are quiet, we know reality itself and not its reflection. However, we must be careful. Sometimes when we sit, it is possible for us to slip the hawser and let go in a way that is but a trick. We slip away from the discipline of questioning, which is our practice. We can then drift into a placid mind-state wherein the mind reflects itself in the mind. Other kinds of practice encourage this placidity, which, from the point of view of Zen practice, is a *cul-de-sac* that should be avoided at all costs. We must avoid this placidity of mind. Unfortunately, because we are so tormented, because we have so much anguish in our lives, when we come up against this state, it tastes so beautiful, so sweet, that we want to linger. But this placid mind-state can quite easily become demonic, giving us an "upside down" view of the truth that can induce a horror of emptiness, of vacuity—a horror of being swallowed by one's own mind.

Go to where the very heart of the problem lies. The heart of the problem lies in the stony, flintlike quality of the mind. This quality very often comes out of an anxiety or an irritation or a discomfort. The mind is uncomfortable with itself or uncomfortable with the world. But in the very center of that discomfort, a crack opens. It is through this crack that you must go. This is not to say that you must make yourself uncomfortable. Please understand this. We are not ascetics. The idea is not to flog yourself, hurt yourself, beat yourself, or anything like that. Just be patient, and life will give you all the misery that you need to work with.

We ask "Who am I?" and against the immensity of the world, we can see ourselves only as "ghosts in the machine." But when we let go of the world as being something immense, and examine what happens when we hear a bird sing or feel the cushion pressing against the leg or see the wall—if we do this without any presuppositions, definitions, or conceptual structures, and we work with the simplicity of sensation—we see that there is no coming together of mind and matter, of "my" seeing the "world," or "my" hearing the "bird." There is no mind. There is no matter. What there is we cannot say. Even to say there is anything is already too much. Reality fills everything. It is impenetrable in its fullness.

Some people want to say that matter exists, but not mind; others that mind exists, but not matter. Others say that the seer and the seen are one. But all this comes from thinking about the problem and not going to the experience itself. The metaphor of the mirror springs to mind. The mirror is not the reflection, the reflection is not the mirror. They are two, yet cannot be separated. Likewise, mind and matter are two but cannot be separated. This is why the Buddhist says no mind (*anatman*), no matter (*anicca*).

The pope has said that Buddhism is too passive and relies too much on detachment. A movement calling for Buddhists to become socially active appeared on the scene not so long ago. This seems to be a lack understanding of detachment on the one hand and a lack of faith on the other, because if Buddhism is not socially active, then what is it? But can we go out and help with the suffering of others until we have ourselves cut out from our own hearts the illusion of separation? If we do so, will not our help simply become another form of fascination? At the bottom, wanting to help others may well come out of a genuine sense of the unity of everything with everything; but at another level it may be just weakness, an unwillingness to face the real issues. The only place we can start to help others is by helping ourselves. There was a very famous Tibetan, Milarepa, who forbade his disciples to go out and help others. He said, "It is only when you can help others without the least element of selfishness that your help can do anything other than end in catastrophe."

Some people, by training, by karma, by temperament, and by nature (such as doctors, psychologists, lawyers), find themselves in situations in which they can do something to ameliorate the suffering of the world. We are not saying that they should stop. What we are talking about is a life philosophy of helping others, a religious requirement to do so. This is what is so disastrous, the belief that we have to interfere with other people's lives because we are Buddhists or Christians or whatever. We do not have the expression "cold as charity" for nothing.

When someone slips, we naturally reach out to support him or her. When someone comes to us in despair, we cannot help holding out our arms to embrace him or her. We do not have to be engaged Buddhists or Christians to do so. The first vow of a Zen Buddhist is to practice to save all sentient beings. But, as Buddha has said, we can do this only when we see there are no sentient beings to save, and no Buddhism to prompt us to save them. This requires detachment, seeing that the mirror is not the reflection, that what a person essentially is, is no different from what I, Buddha, Christ, or whoever essentially is.

We will get rid of war in this world in only one way: by each one of us getting rid of the war in our own hearts. People are not wicked; at heart, none of us is wicked. We are tormented, tormented by ourselves. Unity is turned back against itself. This turning back against itself is the generative or creative force. But it is also the source of destruction and violence, violence being so often failed creativity. The forces that bear on a person are so great, so conflicting, so in opposition to one another, that the normal process of unity and creativity is overwhelmed. In the place of creativity comes a cry, a desperate need to establish something that is reliable, solid, dependable; and out of that cry sometimes comes a fist, an attempt to create something that is stable.

Beyond this war, wherein unity is turned back upon itself, is peace. Someone said, "Peace and silence are my body." He did not mean that this physical flesh, bones and muscle, is peace and silence, but that "peace and silence" *are my body*. This is true of each one of us: peace and silence are our body. Everything is sustained by peace and silence. Everything is sustained, if you like, by love.

One might say that one has one's life to live; its problems, frustrations, and suffering are all very real. How does one deal with this? How can one get rid of the problems? But our problems come out of the situation, and the real question is "How can one step out of the total situation?" not "How can one shuffle the situation around, one part of it against another part of it?" All that does is change one problem for another. Perhaps you do get out of one particular problem, and it is no longer a problem for you; but lo and behold, in solving that one you have created another. Sometimes on the surface this new one is so unrelated to the earlier problem that it is not obvious that it is a direct outcome of solving the first. But dwell on it for a moment and you will often see it is so.

This is why we say that our practice is a matter of intelligence. When you are working, you must work intelligently. You must use the same power that you use if you are a plumber or housewife or doctor or writer; the power you use to deal with these situations is the same power that you use in your practice. The difference is that you are now freeing that power from the forms it normally takes. Usually when one uses this power, it is addressed in a particular way, within a particular limit and a particular form. Instead of trying to find some adequate vehicle for this power, look into the nature of that power itself. As Dogen would say, "Think the unthinkable!"

How often does it happen that people ask, "Why does this have to happen to me? Why do I have all the problems of the world? What is it that I have done? What must I do to escape from all this?" They have the feeling that what is happening to them is an accident and that it could not, indeed should not, have happened. But is it so! What one is faced with is what one is faced with! As long as one believes that one is in the body, sooner or later the insuperable will present itself, even if as a terminal illness.

Someone said, "We seek the real because we are unhappy with the unreal." We are unhappy with the unreal because we are the real. The real is our true nature. We cannot know reality—as long as we are trying to know, see, or grasp reality, we keep returning to the rat race. But we must come to see this truth directly for ourselves. When we come to this truth that we cannot know reality, it comes to us not as negation but as complete affirmation, complete release. Until that release, one has to keep returning to the rat race.

People say to themselves, "I am something": a man, a woman, a mother, a father, a good person, a clever person, and so on. But this "I am something" is itself a derivative. It comes out of what one might call knowing/being or nonreflective awareness. This is our true state, and letting go of the belief in being something is the essence of our practice. This is why we have said many times that our practice is a process. A process in which our practice becomes more and more subtle. This is why we just have to plow on through long periods of dryness, without protest, without trying to justify it, without wanting it to cease—just staying present with it. Breathing it in, breathing it out. Totally there, totally alert. Even when there is a sense of something screaming inside you, just let it scream. Go on. Even when this suddenly gives way and there is a feeling of benediction, just go on.

True happiness includes all sorrow and suffering.

—— · —— · —— · —— · —— · —— · —— · —— · —— · ——

There is in everyone divine power existing in a latent
condition. . . . This one power divided above and below;
generating itself, making itself grow, seeking itself, find-
ing itself, being mother of itself, father of itself, sister of

*itself, spouse of itself, daughter of itself, son of itself—
mother, father, unity, being, a source of the entire circle
of existence.*

—Fourth Patriarch

Chapter Nineteen

Sand Castles

It is like children playing by the sea. All day long they build sand castles with intricate moats and tall battlements. Each one claims a castle as his own. They fight to protect their castles and to pull down the castles of others. They triumph and weep, triumph some more and weep some more. Evening comes; the sun sinks low in the sky. The tide comes in. The children pick up their buckets and spades, turn around, and go home.

The castles sink forgotten beneath the cold waves.

———————————————————————

A new word is like a fresh seed sown on the ground.

———————————————————————

—Ludwig Wittgenstein

PART 4

Sesshin

Introduction to Part Four

An important event in the calendar of a Zen Center is
sesshin, which could be loosely translated as "retreat." At
the Montreal Zen Center we have a sesshin every month except
for July and August, when the weather is too hot and humid.
Sesshins are periods of intense practice and traditionally last for
seven days. At the Zen Center, because we are a lay community
and it is difficult to get a sufficient number of people who are
able to get away from work for seven days to fill a sesshin, we
have only four seven-day sesshins and we have two four-day
and four three-day sesshins. We also have added an extra two-
day sesshin to help introduce newcomers to what *sesshin*
means.

At Montreal we begin a sesshin with an opening ceremony. This takes place during the second period of zazen, or
meditation. During the first period the participants, some of
whom have traveled hundreds of miles, have a chance to settle
in.

The opening ceremony consists of enshrining the figure of
Manjusri and reflecting upon fourteen "reminders." The
enshrinement of Manjusri is accompanied by the four vows,
which are chanted by all the participants. Manjusri is the bodhisattva of *prajna* (wisdom) and presides over the sesshin.
(Prajna is the mind aroused to vigor and discernment.) The
Manjusri that we have is a figure vigorously wielding a sword,
the sword of prajna which it is said cuts in one, not two. In
other figures he is sometimes depicted seated upon a lion. In

this case the lion is a symbol of the kind of tensile energy required in a sesshin. Most of us have seen a lion only in a cage, but even watching its cousin the domestic cat leap to a higher shelf or stalk a bird, one can appreciate the kind of alert, but controlled and dynamic, attitude that is necessary.

The enshrinement of Manjusri is followed by the ceremony of reflecting upon the fourteen reminders. The fourteen reminders were originally written by Thich Nhat Hanh for his community. We have adapted them for use by Westerners and have changed the format from being "commandments" to "reminders." A scholar of Hebrew and the Old Testament told me, by the way, that the Ten Commandments were also originally ten "reminders." We prefer the word *reminders* rather than *precepts* or *commandments* because they are intended to help those participating to arouse the mind that seeks the way. One can no more command or dictate this arousal than one can command or dictate the feeling of love.

As we are a bilingual sangha, the reminders are read by two members of the community: first in French and then in English. Initially, there is an expression of gratitude, and then a chant, "Kanzeon." Kanzeon (in Chinese, *Kuan-yin*) is the bodhisattva of compassion, and we have included this chant to remind us that both wisdom *and* compassion preside over a sesshin. To help underscore this, a figure of the bodhisattva of compassion presides over the room in which are held dokusan, which could be translated as "private interviews."

After the Kanzeon has been chanted, the two readers ask for the community to give spiritual support while the reminders are being read. Then these are read one by one, and a short period of time (about a minute) is given for the group to reflect upon the reminder. It is explained that it is not necessary to *think* about it but rather to give oneself over to the spirit of the reminder.

To end the ceremony, an invocation to Buddhas and bodhisattvas for their aid is read. This sometimes surprises new participants, who ask, "Does Zen rely on outside help? Why should I call upon nonexistent Buddhas for help that I do not need?" Calling upon Buddhas and bodhisattvas and asking for their aid is a reminder that the ego, which thinks it is in control, is but a figment of the delusory mind. While it is true there are no Buddhas "out there," so it is true that there is no self [I] "in here." The self and the Other, the self and the Buddha, although not the same, are nevertheless two aspects of one seamless whole.

After the invocation to Buddhas and bodhisattvas, we chant the repentance *gatha*. This is intended to give ourselves the opportunity to lay down some of the burden of regret, remorse, and guilt that it is the lot of human beings to carry through life.

The ceremony ends with three prostrations. It is explained to newcomers that although we face the Buddha (or in this case, the Manjusri figure) to make prostrations, they are not gestures of adoration to Buddha or Manjusri. The prostrations are gestures of humility; one comes down to earth. By prostrating, to use the phrase of a master, we lower the mast of ego.

Each day we have a chanting service in the afternoon. This service includes the Prajnaparamita, the Kanzeon, and the four vows. We also have chanting before meals. Eating is much more than providing fuel for the body; throughout most societies it is a way of uniting a group. The business lunch is but the latest in ritualized eating. Possibly the most celebrated example of what I mean is the mass held in commemoration of the Last Supper. Chanting also has a harmonizing and unifying value.

In the chants the sangha declares "We take this food to attain the Buddha Way" and so affirms that eating the food should express their ardent desire to free themselves of the obstructions of thoughts about self. At the same time the chants give an opportunity to express gratitude to all the countless beings who have contributed to providing the meal. The last part of the chanting service is devoted to "hungry and thirsty ghosts." This expression, "hungry and thirsty ghosts," can be interpreted in a number of ways, one being that the ghosts represent all those parts of the mind that hover in the shadows during sesshin, afraid to participate but unable to leave.

Ravaged by thirst and hunger, the expression of greed and lust, they are never at rest, and the chant and its accompanying offerings are devoted to giving them peace.

Dokusan, or private interview, is held twice a day during sesshin. Generally speaking, only students come to dokusan during sesshin, and almost all are working on one koan or another. Dokusan is very important for a number of reasons, and most students come at every available opportunity. We continue to use the Japanese word *dokusan* because we have no English equivalent. "Interview" suggests counseling, and although counseling is given, it is not the primary aim of dokusan.

A third feature of sesshin is *teisho*. This is another Japanese word that we continue to use for want of an appropriate English equivalent. Translators often use "sermon," but insofar as sermons often have a moral exhortation as their basis, the term is quite unsuitable. "Talk" is too casual because a teisho is an intense, lively presentation. "Lecture" suggests conveying information of one kind or another, and although information is sometimes conveyed, this is incidental to the purpose of the teisho, which is a heart-to-heart communion.

At Montreal, following the tradition established at the Rochester Zen Center, a teisho may have as its basis some text of a master, and we often use Nisargadatta's *I am that* for this purpose, or a koan. Normally texts are read and commented upon during the first half of a sesshin, and koans during the second half. The talks included in Part One are talks that have been transcribed from recordings made during sesshin. This section includes some transcriptions of teishos on koans. Unfortunately, when a teisho is transcribed, its life is lost. A teisho, particularly a teisho on koans, is meant to arouse the mind that seeks the way. Someone likened it to striking sparks off the *hara*. However, some teishos are included that have been edited and expanded for general consumption.

A koan is a saying and sometimes an action of a Zen master. In order to work with a koan, one must work from one's own awakened state. In other words, one works from the faith "I am whole and complete" and then asks oneself how the koan expresses this truth. Some koans originated with a novice asking for direction from a Zen master. Others come from a monk wanting to test his own level of penetration against a Zen master. Others come from two highly developed monks, nuns, or masters who are simply whetting their dharma swords. These latter are called *dharma combat* or *dharma duels*. One must not take the word *combat* too seriously, as it is as much a dharma dance, like the flamenco dance, as it is a combat.

In our tradition we have about two hundred koans to work on, and koan practice splits clearly into two parts: before and after kensho. The koan one works on before kensho is called a *breakthrough koan*. A breakthrough koan requires immense effort and dedication. By "effort," I do not mean physical but spiritual effort. The mind is asleep, or under a spell, and must be awakened. In modern society in particular, everything is dedicated toward maintaining one in the sleep state. Television is perhaps the worst culprit in this regard. It is well known that the object of a television program is not to entertain so much as to put the viewer into a state of mind receptive to the advertisements that follow. Furthermore, the kind of program that one views is determined by demand based upon ratings, and most people want to sleep. Apart from television there are also newspapers and journals whose function is to inform but also to shock. Normally the newspaper has some political bias and so often uses its pages to influence people in one direction or another. Novels, films, and plays are also sleep-inducing mechanisms. One of the more alarming trends in industry is the trend in which newcomers to the workforce require that work should be "fun." All this adds to the burden of anyone seriously wanting to undertake spiritual work.

The breakthrough that one works for when working on a koan is kensho or satori. Kensho has been widely misunderstood both by its advocates and by its detractors. One big confusion that can occur is that between "resolving" the koan and seeing into one's true nature. Resolving a koan of itself is of no particular value, any more than understanding the sutras at an intellectual or even intuitive level has any lasting value. I often say to people practicing at the Center not to come to practice

Zen. "To practice Zen" means that one enters into a system with its own rules and rewards, without necessarily having contact with other aspects of life. One can become a "good" Zen Buddhist in the same way that one can become a good member of the Kiwanis Club, the Jaycees, and so on. Being a good Zen Buddhist would then often mean regular attendance at evening meditation and sesshin and a good batch of "answers" to koans that one has worked on.

Seeing into one's own nature itself is also misunderstood in that it is often associated with the immediate acquisition of abilities, qualities, and powers that one did not have before the awakening. People who are awakened are expected to be models of compassion, self-control, wisdom, and so on. Even if these expectations are not felt, it is nevertheless felt that in some way people who come to awakening should be special. I am told that sometimes after a sesshin in Japan the people who have come to awakening parade around the zendo, while at other times (even for a while at the center where I was trained) they are awarded a special insignia called a rakusu.

Some people who teach and practice Zen maintain that kensho is not even necessary, pointing out that the ambition it can arouse in people is a liability that need not be incurred. Unfortunately, this is even extended further to say that awakening is not only unnecessary but unattainable and that sitting in zazen is already sufficient. This is a grave mistake. Kensho is possible, not only for the Easterner but for the Westerner also. Not only is it possible, but it is the heart of Buddhist teaching and is what is of value to the Westerner in that teaching. The Buddhist teaching on ethics and the subtleties of Buddhist philosophy are in no way superior to what the West has to offer. It is not necessary to go to Buddhism for ethical guidance. However, we no longer have a tradition of personal experience of the truth mainly because the Church insists on its being the intermediary. In the past there was in Christianity a living tradition of personal and direct experience, and we have previously made reference to some of this tradition. But this has to a large extent been lost.

To see into one's own nature is to see that one is beyond

all form. It is not necessary to *be something* to know, or *know something* to be. This is the great teaching of Buddha. It is this that all the koans express in one way or another. Basic to Zen practice is the Prajna Paramita, and the core of this teaching is that *form is emptiness and emptiness is form.* The "is" is not the "is" of identity, and the first koan that is included is a commentary on this in a very poetic way.

To come to awakening, one must come down to earth. One must be ordinary. A basic drive in life is the drive to be unique, special. This drive not only is a human drive but is to be found in animals as well. It may well be the fullest expression of the need to survive. To come to spiritual maturity, one must transcend this need to be unique, go beyond it. In practice this means that one must first let go of all one's desires for the absolute: the absolutely good, the absolutely true and holy, the absolute self. Buddha's teaching was provisional, and he insisted that it was necessary to transcend this teaching also. As one lets go of the need for the absolute, so one is able to accept the ordinary. The absolute gives one a taste of the exquisite. When one seeks after the absolute but is denied it, the exquisite becomes first the bitter and then the sour. But even these are better than the insipid, the taste that accompanies the ordinary. The celebrated Zen master Pai-chang said there were three secrets at his monastery: drink tea, take care, and rest. He said, "If you still try to think any more about them, I know you are still not through." The second koan that we have chosen epitomizes the humility necessary to be able to practice.

The most troubling of all problems in life is the problem of death, and yet this problem—if faced with humility—is one that can deepen practice like nothing else can. In other words, our greatest enemy in life can be our greatest friend in practice. To help in understanding this, we include a koan on death.

Chapter Twenty

A Sesshin

A sesshin—the orchestration of twenty-five minds; the coming together of yearnings and strivings, piercing questions and dumb perplexity; the pooling of patience and pain; the sacrifice of exertion to attain one knows not what for one knows not why. Each bears the full responsibility for all. In a unification of mind, in the clear openness of mindless seeking beyond thought, beyond the thought of thought, the sesshin finds its focus. In the strangling despair, in the dryness, in the probing with a nerveless hand that can no longer grasp nor let go, in the pointlessness, the sesshin finds its temper. Go on, just go on, just keep going on, on, on, ON! There is a pulsing that is deeper than the pulsing of breathing, an inevitable pulsing that builds silent cadence upon silent cadence. It is called *joriki*—it is the energy of the sesshin. Concentration, unification, samadhi—and then the last step. *Sesshin* literally means in Japanese "to unify or concentrate the mind." It also means to search the mind, but in practice *sesshin* means a time when the "the fire and rose are one."

Eyes down, back erect, legs crossed or kneeling, hands held with the left one resting palm up on the right, thumbs not quite touching, not quite separate. No moving! For thirty-five minutes you are alone with yourself, with no way to escape. You cannot leave the sesshin. The tension builds. After thirty-five minutes, five minutes' walking zazen. A measured, sturdy walk, not a walk as a stroll or even as a march: an unobstructed walking, a steady lifting of the legs and putting them down, one after the other. Again zazen, again the claustrophobia.

Even those who have sat for years are moved by the solemnity of the opening ceremony, the enshrinement of Manjusri, the toll of the large bell, and the reading of the fourteen reminders. It is as though a great iron gate is lowered, severing one from all that would interrupt or interfere, from all that would seduce and offer an alternative, an excuse, a "better" way. Even some of those who have sat for years sweat the sweat of the committed; to those who have sat but for a short time, at first can come surges of panic, a feeling that all is lost. But from the very beginning, the sesshin—the togetherness and unification of minds—gives a support to all, and the steady work of those with experience meets the inspired working of those for whom the sesshin is the first, and in this meeting the first doubts subside, the participants settle down, the sesshin gets under way.

"There are some important guidelines to the sesshin." It is the teacher talking. After the opening ceremony, after the bows and prostrations, the teacher addresses the sesshin. "The first is silence. You must remain silent at all times. There must be no talking or whispering. If you must communicate, do so by note and do so out of the view of others. This is a most important guideline. Next, keep your eyes down at all times. Do not give way to negative thoughts. Remember, everyone who comes does so at some considerable personal sacrifice. You have a responsibility not only to yourself but to everyone else present also. Finally, do your utmost—strive with all your energies and do not give way to discouragement." At this stage the teacher may well add a favorite story of the Chinese master who said, "If you set a time limit for success in Zen training, then you should act like a man who has fallen into a thousand-foot-deep pit. His thousand and ten thousand thoughts are reduced to a single thought: how to escape from the pit. He keeps it up from morning to evening and from evening to morning. If you train in this way and do not realize the Truth in five or seven days, may I burn in hell for deceiving you."

In the well of silence of seven days—the silence of twenty-five people who have agreed to allow their normal compensations and barriers to loosen and who have agreed to let the pain of their human sickness ooze, flow, and surge up—the One Mind is seen. It is not a silence of absence but a silence of presence. It is the silence of which all things are made, a silence of moods: expectation, anxiety, urgency, deep peace, and despair. It is the silence of deep breathing and of the crack of the kyosaku. It is the silence of weeping, laughing, roaring. It is the silent heart of the sesshin; it is the silent heart of us all.

With the eyes down, images are not made; when images are not made, the mind's froth is undisturbed. At first how hard! What a temptation it is to give way to the aching pleasure of looking at things. The falling snow, the new leaves, the flooding sunlight, the rustling leaves, suck and draw at the peripheral vision; but give way even once and the fountain dries up and "the pale cast of thought" dries hard. Keeping silent and keeping the eyes down—two simple rules, but out of them come the heart and mind of the sesshin.

In the beginning pain presides. It starts on the first day and nags, twists, scorches, and tears throughout the next seven; physical pain, pain in the legs, the ankles, knees, hips; pain in the shoulders, in the neck; headache and backache. And then that other more immediate pain, the pain of frustration, humiliation, and shame—how is it such ordinary foolishness of so many years past can thus wrench at our fibers?—the pain of emptiness, fear, and dread; the pain of stupidity as the koan sticks there, a meaningless phrase; the pain of the kyosaku; and worst of all, the pain of others. But we have tried comfort. All our lives we squirmed into greater warmth, snuggled into the cozy corner, twisted away from truth, and smothered the protesting voice. All our lives we have heeded the common crowd and tranquilized our torment until the tranquilizer becomes our torment and our escape becomes its own form of prison. And so here we are. We need to know, we must find out; so pain is inevitable. "All is suffering," the first noble truth, is a truth without doubt to those in sesshin. Pain is the fire of sesshin. If it is gold, it will never burn; if it burns, it was never gold. But without pain, no burning burns; and without burning, no release into home is possible. "Become one with pain!" and the protest is let slip, the tension relaxes, only pain remains; and then no pain, just energy, untapped reservoirs of energy. The dryness is gone, the doubting is gone, just white-hot energy; but don't wobble, whatever you do.

The sesshin rolls on. A round of sitting, breakfast, work, rest, zazen, teisho, zazen, lunch, zazen, chanting, exercise, zazen, supper, zazen, zazen, zazen. And behind it all like some backdrop is dokusan. The tinkling summons of the teacher's bell calls out, and the sonorous "I come" of the dokusan bell responds. Here is the burr under the saddle, the balm, the goad, the beckoning. So much patience, so much faith. It is pointless to pretend. The room is so quiet that any attempt to dissimulate, to evade, to puff up, clangs and echoes. "The truth is I don't know who or what I am, what I'm supposed to do. Wherever I am is the wrong place. I'm like an axle without grease, a wheel off center." Question, probe, encouragement, now a story, now a reminiscence, more questions, more probes. How can he have faith in something so wooden and unresponding? Ting-a-ling-a-ling, dong dong; ting-a-ling-a-ling, dong dong. Afternoon and evening. Patience and faith.

Dokusan is one of the pillars of sesshin, zazen another, and teisho the third. "Today we shall work on koan number. . . ." Every day comes teisho. The koan is the kernel, but around it is wrapped the fruit of experience ripened through long years of practice. In a teisho one knows that every word has been paid for. There are none of the verbal excesses of the spendthrift. There are often humor and drama, sometimes poetry, but always a pointedness. A wide range is covered—background material, admonishments, insights, descriptions, encouragement. It is like a cubist painting that has its own perspective. It should all hang together and make sense.

Before you know it, the sixth day has arrived. The first day is somehow easy. One lives off the impact of everyday life, and a merciful soporific lies in that impact. The second day is harder, and the third is somehow the hardest of all. In the early years, to wake up on the third day is to surface through black tar. The very dregs of the ego are encountered, and these dregs cling and clog the mind, the head aches and the limbs rebel at the posture; the cushions, the tan, the stick, rebel at it all. But now it is the sixth day, and for a while it is like passing through a meadow. Vast space, cool breeze, sunshine, and peace. The rebellion, the black tar, the pain, have somehow evaporated, and for a time everything is easy. Now is the great testing time. Shall I rest, shall I sit down here, shall I wait awhile? I must sit down just for a while.

The seventh night, the violet hour. It is time to stand up and walk home, to walk through walls and barriers, through archaic obstacles; now the hundred-foot Buddha is born. With dignity of great purpose *kinhin* revolves: the hands, the feet, the set mouth. Steadfast the feet take up a beat—many feet but one beat, many hands but one grasp. The One Mind revolves in the violet hour of the seventh night.

And then it is over. Music laughs out loud. The embraces, the tears, the laughter, the wonder, and gratitude. What happened to the giants? These are ordinary people after all. Wonderful, wonderful. What do you say to someone with whom you have sat for a week (or was it an eternity?), whom you've come to know in a way that is hard to believe and impossible to describe? What does your right hand say to your left? The tongue is thick and clumsy, and it's best said with a look, a smile, a hug. A seven-day sesshin—the orchestration of twenty-five minds.

_ . _ . _ . _ . _ . _ . _ . _ . _ . _ . _ . _ . _

Life, like a dome of many colored glass,
Stains the white radiance of eternity.
_ . _ . _ . _ . _ . _ . _ . _ . _ . _ . _ . _

—Shelley

Chapter Twenty-One

The Fourteen Reminders

Incense Offering

In gratitude we offer this incense to all Buddhas in the ten directions. May its fragrance pervade our lives through our careful efforts, wholehearted awareness, and slowly ripening understanding. May we and all beings be companions of Buddhas and bodhisattvas. May we awaken from forgetfulness and realize our true home.

Introduction

Today I have been asked by the community to read the fourteen reminders. I beg the community for spiritual support. Please, sisters and brothers, listen with a serene mind. Let us use these fourteen reminders as a source of inspiration to arouse correct endeavor. Let us reflect on each reminder as a way to harmony and unity, both with others and in ourselves.

The First Reminder

Let us not idolize or be bound to any doctrine, theory, or ideology, including those of Buddhism. Let us see all systems of thought as guiding means and not as absolute truth.

The Second Reminder

Let us not believe the knowledge we currently possess to be changeless, absolute truth. Let us avoid being narrow-minded and bound to present views. Let us learn and practice the open way of nonattachment from views and be open to receive others' viewpoints.

THE THIRD REMINDER

Let us not misuse authority, money, education, or other means to force others, including children, to adopt our viewpoint. Through compassionate dialogue let us help ourselves and others to renounce fanaticism and narrowness.

THE FOURTH REMINDER

Let us not avoid contact with suffering or close our eyes to suffering. Let us be mindful of the existence of suffering in the world. Let us find ways to be with and comfort those who are suffering.

THE FIFTH REMINDER

Let us not accumulate wealth while millions are hungry. Let us not take as the aim of our life fame, profit, wealth, or sensual pleasure. Let us live simply and share our time with those who are in need. Let us not be wasteful of food, the work of others, or time.

THE SIXTH REMINDER

Let us not nurture anger or hatred. Let us see how it arises out of separation and seek early reconciliation to restore harmony and unity. Let us be compassionate toward ourselves and others.

THE SEVENTH REMINDER

Let us not lose ourselves through identifying with all that happens, but use the energy of practice to help us constantly remember ourselves.

THE EIGHTH REMINDER

Let us not say things that can create discord and cause division in the community. Let us do our utmost to reconcile and resolve all conflicts, however small they may be.

THE NINTH REMINDER

Let us not say untruthful things or spread gossip for the sake of personal gain or to impress others. Let us not criticize or condemn things that we are unsure of, but always speak truthfully and constructively. Let us nevertheless have the courage to speak out against injustice even when it may threaten our own well-being.

THE TENTH REMINDER

Let us not use the Buddhist community for personal gain or profit nor transform the community into a political party. Let us respect the buildings and land of the community as a place for sacred endeavor.

THE ELEVENTH REMINDER

Let us not pursue a vocation harmful to human beings or nature. Let us not support activities that deprive other beings of their chance to life. Let us, as far as possible, have a vocation that does not run counter to our ideals of compassion.

THE TWELFTH REMINDER

Let us not kill and, where possible, let us prevent others from killing. Let us use whatever means possible to protect life and prevent war.

THE THIRTEENTH REMINDER

Let us not take things that belong to others, but respect the property of others. Let us endeavor to dissuade others from using human suffering to enrich themselves.

THE FOURTEENTH REMINDER

Let us treat our body with respect and not misuse it nor treat it simply as an object. Let us use sexual expression as a means of love and commitment and be aware of the suffering that its misuse may cause ourselves and others. Let us be fully aware of the responsibility of bringing new lives into the world.

Brothers and sisters, I have read aloud the fourteen reminders as the community has wished. Let us be grateful for the opportunity at the beginning of this sesshin to reflect together upon these fourteen reminders.

INVOCATION TO BUDDHAS AND BODHISATTVAS

We ask the Buddhas and patriarchs who have come to awakening to free us from obstructive suffering, the legacy of our past lives, and to help us share in the merit power that fills the countless worlds. The Buddhas and patriarchs in the past were like us, and we shall in the future become Buddhas and patriarchs.

REPENTANCE GATHA

All evil actions committed by me since time immemorial, stemming from greed, anger, and ignorance, arising from body, speech, and mind, I now repent having committed.

THE FOUR VOWS

All beings without number,
I vow to liberate;
Endless blind passions,
I vow to uproot;
Dharma gates without number,
I vow to penetrate;
The great Way of Buddha,
I vow to attain.

Chapter Twenty-Two

Chosha Goes for a Walk

The Case

One day, Chosha went for a walk. When he returned to the gate, the head monk asked, "Master, where have you been strolling?" Chosha replied, "I have come from walking in the hills." The head monk repeated, "But where have you been?" Chosha said, "First I went following the fragrant grasses; now I have returned in pursuit of the falling blossoms." The monk exclaimed, "How much like the springtime you seem to be." And Chosha said, "It is better even than the autumn dews falling on the lotus leaves." Another master interpolated, "Thanks for your reply."

Verse

> *The world without a speck of dust.*
> *Whose eyes are not opened?*
> *First following the fragrant grasses,*
> *Returning in pursuit of falling blossoms,*
> *The slender stork perched in the wintry tree,*
> *A crazed monkey shrieking on the age-old heights.*
> *Chosha's eternal meaning. Ah!*

Chosha, a successor to Nansen, was a famous Zen master in his day. His teaching, much like Nansen's and Joshu's, was not fire and brimstone, although (as will be seen in a moment) he could be quite forceful. Zen masters like Rinzai and Unmon used to induce a state of crisis and tension to get their monks to practice deeply, but Chosha used the natural contradictions of the mind to fuel the practice. Each teacher has his or her own style, which depends upon their training and temperament. Some teachers are very physical, others more intellectual, still others are poetic, and so on. It is essential that a teacher be true to his or her own style and not try to copy the style of another.

A master is not someone you can classify very easily, and often he or she will act out of character. An exchange that occurred between Chosha and his student, Yangshan, when they were sitting enjoying the moon, provides an example. Sitting watching the moon is very calming and peaceful. The sky at night, with the moon, has a quality that is expansive, endless. In deep samadhi, beyond all things and thought, it is just as though bright moonlight shines on a vast dark, empty plain. In Zen circles, therefore, the moon is often looked upon as representing the true self. The great circle that Zen masters sometimes draw echoes the moon. Japanese haiku poets wrote extensively about it. To give just one example:

> Autumn's bright moon,
> however far I have walked, still afar off
> in an unknown sky[1]

To return to the exchange, Yangshan and Chosha were sitting enjoying the moon. And Yangshan points to it and said, "Everyone has it, it's just that they cannot use it." The question naturally arises, What does he mean by this? Hakuin in his verse on zazen says, "From the beginning, all beings are Buddha." We are all awakened; we just aren't able to see this truth. All that is necessary is a turnabout; nothing in particular needs to change. But with this turnabout, or *pravritti*, everything is changed. Chosha agreed we all have it, "True, this is so." And then he asked, "What about your using it?" In other words, show me your awakening. Yangshan shot back, "Well, you use it yourself." This was not a good reply, and Chosha knocked him over with a single blow. This blow both demonstrated the use of it, and at the same time gave Yangshan a lesson. Yangshan got up and said, "Respected uncle, you're just like a tiger." That is how Chosha got his name; it means "tiger."

Everyone has it, they just don't know how to use it.

Chosha once gave a talk in which he said, "If I were to thoroughly uphold the teaching of our sect, there would be weeds a fathom deep in the teaching hall." In other words, "If I were to try to say all that could be said about Zen, the whole place would be full of dead words." "Weeds," "clinging to weeds," or "falling in the weeds" mean excess verbiage, excess talk and words. "But," he went on, "even so, I cannot help telling you that the entire world is reflected by the eye of the monk, the entire world is contained in everyday conversation, the entire world is throughout your body, the entire world is your own divine light, the entire world is within your divine light, and the entire world is inseparable from yourself." Christ, when he speaks of himself as "the light of the world," seems to be saying something similar to Chosha's saying, "the entire world is your own divine light."

Chosha also said, "The entire world is inseparable from yourself." Awareness and the world are inseparable. Yet although the world is inseparable from me, this does not mean the world is the same as me. "Awareness as" the world is like a mirror in which the world is reflected; the reflection in a mirror is inseparable from the mirror, but mirror and reflection are not the same. When we see our face reflected in the mirror, we tend to forget the mirror and instead see the reflection as real on its own, just as when we look "at" the world, we forget that we are looking at awareness as the world and instead see the world as something existing on its own, independently of us.

Again to quote Chosha, "The entire world is reflected by the eye of the monk." Although we might use the expression "I am aware," this is not strictly true because awareness is *already* "I am"; awareness and "I am" are not two. The whole world is not cold and abstract but essentially personal; the whole world is "I am." The whole world is awareness. Christianity expresses this in the personhood of God; in Buddhism, in the idea of the Cosmic Buddha. Buddha says, "Throughout heaven and earth, I alone am the honored one." This doesn't mean that throughout the whole cosmos there is no one who is not Siddhartha Gautama. Siddhartha Gautama too is part of the cosmos. The "I am" of Buddha is the same "I am" of Christ when he says, "I am the light of the world." The expression "throughout heaven and earth" means the "whole world," and "I alone am the honored one" refers to "the eye of the monk." In other words, the monk—and therefore each of us—can also say with Siddhartha Gautama, "Throughout heaven and earth, I alone am the honored one." Each of us has it.

This is the kind of mystery that truly our everyday language and our everyday way of thinking are unable to contain. When the Japanese Zen master Hakuin came to great awakening, he exclaimed "I am Ganto." Ganto, a Zen master, had cried out at his death, and this had given Hakuin a life koan: how was it possible that a Zen master could cry out like that at his death? Hakuin resolved the koan when he cried out, "I am Ganto." But, one might well ask, how can "I am" of Buddha, "I am" of Christ, "I am" of Hakuin, and "I am" of Ganto be the same? When you say "I am" and I say "I am," we *say* something different, but does that mean that what inspires us to say "I am" must be different? Each of us has it, and it is no different.

Each of a great number of puddles reflects the moon. The puddles are the personalities of Jesus, Siddhartha, Hakuin, Ganto, you, and me. Because each puddle reflects the moon, it is "alive," "conscious," and alive and conscious in its own way: this is a big puddle, that a small one, this deep, that shallow, this muddy, that clear. A puddle dries up and so does not reflect the moon any more, and we say it is dead. Then it rains again, and the puddle returns and again reflects the moon, so we say the puddles have been reborn.

Each puddle reflects the whole moon; the whole moon is contained in each puddle. But there is only one moon. Each of us is that one moon. Each is that one moon in its entirety. From the beginning, as Hakuin says, "All beings are Buddha." Each of us has it. Even though the wind blows and ruffles the water, as the haiku poet says,

> The moon in the water;
> broken and broken again,
> still it is there.[2]

We break up the whole into separate units and fix each with a word, such as "hills," "fields," "grass," "lotus leaves," "spring," "autumn." Because of this we come to believe that we are something among other things in the world, and other people are in opposition to us. We know only multiplicity; and the unity that is the source and origin escapes us. Yet, our language and thought too insist upon unity; as Chosha said, "The entire world is contained in everyday conversation." Language revolves around the idea that everything is equal to itself, everything is one, everything is an identity. By the use of logic, we generalize this and say $A=A$, everything equals itself. Even so, life is beyond all verbal description, all logical understanding, and mathematical formulation, hence, the joy that is released when we allow "one and multiplicity": know the multiplicity in the one, and the one in the multiplicity.

Chosha went on to say, "I always tell you people that the Buddhas of the triple world, the cosmos, and the mass of living beings are the light of great perfect wisdom." This light is *bodhi,* knowing. And he asked, "When the light has not yet shone forth, where can you people turn to become intimately acquainted with it?" Someone asked Joshu a similar question, "What happens when the light does not shine?" And Joshu said, "You have betrayed yourself." We betray ourselves constantly when we search around wanting to become awakened. Hakuin says we are "like one in water crying, I 'thirst.' " Chosha echoed this, saying, "Before the light shines forth there isn't even any news of Buddhas or sentient beings, and where would we get the mountains, rivers, and the earth?" But even so, everything is showing this light shining forth.

At that time a monk asked Chosha, "What is the monk's eye?" The master said, "Never, ever can one depart from it. Those who have attained Buddhahood and become patriarchs cannot depart from it. The six powers of transmigration cannot depart from it." Even though you fall into the deepest hell, you are still within the eye of the monk, the eye that never closes.

The monk persisted and asked, "What is it they cannot depart from?" The master replied, "In daytime, seeing the sun;

at night, seeing the stars." Everything that you can see is it, and this means not only seeing with your eyes but seeing with your ears, and with your fingertips. One *is* seeing, one *is* knowing. Knowing and the world—the sun in the daytime, the stars at night—are inseparable. The monk said, "I still don't understand." And the master said, "Marvelous towering mountains, their color blue upon blue."

Everything right there; look at it, immense, immense, immense. How can you not see it? How can you not see it? A Christian monk said, "Oh, my God, how is it that in this poor world, thou who art so great cannot be found by anyone? Thou who art so near cannot be felt, thou who gives thyself to everyone, yet no one knows thy name." How is it? Right before your eyes, it is your eyes; it's the substance of your eyes.

A monk asked Chosha, "Who is the teacher of all Buddhas?"

And Chosha said, "By whom has he been concealed?"

Let us go now to the koan. A koan gives expression to the awakened state, and to work with a koan, you must work from the awakened condition. In the koan, Chosha goes for a walk. When most people go for a walk, they walk *through* the fields and woods or whatever, and these fields and woods "are out there." And they move *through* them and come back *from* them. One even has the same illusion when one goes to the cinema, particularly if it is an Imax cinema with the huge screen on which films are projected to give the illusion of movement. After a while you forget that you are looking at a film and feel that you are moving through the landscape. Sometimes the film is about a roller coaster that goes up and down at a fair, and you feel that you are on this roller coaster going up and down with it. But, of course, neither you nor the screen goes anywhere: the illusion of movement is just that, an illusion of movement. It is like walking toward a mirror. The reflection does not move, the mirror and the reflection are inseparable. So it is when you walk through the fields: you lend yourself to the walk, you give yourself over to the "reality" of the movement of the walking. You admire the countryside *out there* and say how beautiful *it* is, how wonderful the view is, how peaceful it all seems, and so on.

But this peaceful view—and the beauty, whatever it might be—is a reflection. If, in the quiet of the countryside, you listen to the sound of a cricket and then switch back and forth between the sound and the silence, you see that sound and silence are not opposites but rather that sound gives form to silence. It is almost as though the sound is the incarnation of the silence. The silence is not absent; it is not that you hear sound and so silence is absent, and then silence comes and so sound is absent. When you listen to the sound, you still hear the silence. And when you listen to the silence, you hear the sound, but it loses its substance in some way—it becomes more ghostlike.

It is the same with seeing; everything we see is stillness incarnate, not only what we see but what we feel as well. When we feel sad or angry or bored, we lose the stillness; but if we return to the stillness, the emotions lose their fire, their passion, in the same way that objects lose their solidity. At a deeper level still, we can say that the self is the form given to the no-self. And when we are the self, the no-self is lost; but when we return to the no-self, then the self loses its grip, and it is as though one dreams.

The koan says: One day, Chosha went for a walk. When he returned to the gate, the head monk asked, "Master, where have you been strolling?"

This is a classic question of a master, "Where are you from?" In another koan Zen master Ummon asks a monk, Tozan, "Where are you from?" Tozan answers, "Oh, I'm from such-and-such a monastery," and Ummon went on, "How long were you there?" and Tozan replied, "About six months." "And what were you doing there?" " I was doing a retreat," and so on, and then all of a sudden Ummon explodes and kicks Tozan out, shouting, "You're just a lot of rubbish; what the hell are you wasting my time for? Go! Beat it! Go on! Scram!" Mumon, the compiler, says in his commentary, "Now, I want to ask you, should Tozan have been beaten or not? If you say yes, then what you are saying is that the whole world should be beaten. If you say no, then are you saying that Ummon is a fool and a bully?"

Chosha was a deeply awakened Zen master and yet he said in reply to the head monk's question, "I have come from walking in the hills," giving, more or less, the same kind of response that Tosan gave. To understand this reply, you must remember what was said about the interplay between self and no-self; between stillness and form, sound and silence; between mirror and reflection. You have to keep both in mind. This is true with all koans.

All religious teaching use parables, symbols, stories, and metaphors as teaching devices. Christ talks about sheep, seeds, fishing, and so on. The Sufis have stories about Mullah Nasr Eddin, and the Hindus stories about Krishna. Western occultism is full of symbolism. All these stories and symbols propel you into a nonliteral, nonlogical realm, the intermediate realm of the mirror and its reflection, silence and sound. However, when working with a koan, in addition to being propelled into a nonliteral, nonlogical realm, you must also work from the awakened state. Where are you from? Where have you been? A haiku of Basho says:

No one
walks along this path
this autumn evening.

The head monk repeated, "But where have you been?" In other words, he's off balance. He was expecting to get an awakened reply, but all he got was a factual, everyday statement. It is just like when Joshu, who at the time was still a novice, asked Zen master Nansen, "What is the way?" Nansen replied, "Everyday mind is the way." Later still in the same encounter he added, "It is like vast space." But what does Nansen mean by saying everyday mind is like vast space? Most people find it claustrophobic, frustrating, limiting, not at all like vast space! And yet Nansen said, "It is like vast space." This is the twist and is the heart of the koan. Chosha is more poetic, but he's saying the same thing: "First I went following the fragrant grasses; now I have returned in pursuit of the falling blossoms."

I wonder how many people of today have really experienced the fragrant grasses? When I was young most of the work was done by horses because cars and trucks were relatively scarce. Hay was an important commodity. Whole fields would be given over to growing grass and cutting, and stacking hay was an important part of a farmer's work. Walking through the fields in an English countryside that was full of fragrant cut grass aroused pure wonder. It is like vast space; it is not me *and* the grass, but me *as* the grass. When Chosha said, "First I went following the fragrant grasses," you have to understand him as you understand the haiku "No one walks along this path": total involvement, a Oneness. But not the Oneness of identity. It is the Oneness of twoness. It is the Oneness that comes from remembering oneself, that comes from being the mirror and at the same time allowing the reflections to be.

It is the same with ". . . now I have returned in pursuit of the falling blossoms." The Japanese have a particular thing for falling blossoms, for the poignancy of a blossom falling. A whole universe crashes, in a way. But when the flower falls . . . it just falls. It just falls; that is all you can say about it. The fall is the utter essence of simplicity. "I have returned in pursuit of the falling blossoms" means that whereas before I was lost in the Oneness of the vastness of fragrant grasses, I am now immersed in the Oneness of total simplicity. A falling blossom reveals the utter nakedness of Oneness, of simplicity—the absolute no "thereness" as the blossom falls. So, in other words, Chosha gave the monk what he expected, but not in the way the monk might have expected it.

"Where have you been strolling?" "I have come from walking in the hills." On the face of it, this is just a mundane, ordinary statement; but coming from a Zen master, while remaining a mundane ordinary statement, it changes completely.

The monk went on to say, "How much like the springtime you seem to be." Chosha replied, "It is better even than the autumn dews falling on the lotus leaves." To understand these two statements, "How very much like the springtime" and "It is better even than the autumn dews falling on the lotus leaves," you must be aware of the feeling that Japanese people had about autumn, which is summed up by two Japanese words, *sabi* and *wabi*.

Sabi is a feeling of loneliness, of melancholy—a feeling that pervades the haiku "No one walks along this path this autumn evening." It has a feeling of being alone, lonely. This is not loneliness accompanied by a lurking fear that many know so well. Sabi has an "all one" quality, and "all one" is the etymology of *alone*. R. H. Blyth says that sabi comes from "to rust" with the feeling of the passage of time. Autumn is essentially a lonely time. It is a time when leaves fall, bringing home the truth that time is passing; in autumn one is poignantly aware of time passing in a way that one isn't at other times of the year. Summer has an eternal quality about it, so has winter, at least in Quebec. Loneliness and melancholy, the sense of passing time, of impermanence, and beyond it all, Unity, is the sabi quality.

The other aspect, wabi, is pure poverty, bareness. "Blessed are the poor in spirit" is the essence of wabi and of zazen. In koan number ten of the Mumonkan a monk, Seizei, said to Zen master Sozan, "I'm poor and destitute; I beg you, give me some sustenance." This poverty is wabi. Wabi too is peculiarly applicable to autumn. Austerity and poverty, it is true, are also applicable to winter, but autumn has a transitional aspect, a sabi aspect, and so the poverty of autumn is not so austere. Springtime, on the other hand, is the time of burgeoning life: it is fullness, richness, the opposite of wabi. And insofar as new life bursts into being, time is on the side of life. Autumn is just the opposite . . . you know when you are getting old, you talk about it as being the autumn of your life. And time is certainly not on your side anymore.

Here are a few haiku that help give you the feeling evoked in the Japanese by autumn:

The long, fall footsteps
are distant
on the autumn leaves.

When somebody is coming to meet you, whereas he would normally clump, clump, clump along, now because leaves have fallen, his footsteps are muffled, distant. The muffled quality makes them somehow seem farther away, which accentuates the loneliness of autumn. Another haiku gives the wabi quality:

The autumn wind goes right through
into the very bones
of the scarecrow.

The autumn wind, as you know, can be biting. The poet has become one with the scarecrow. He shares the poverty of the scarecrow, with its inability to stop the passage of the autumn wind, but he also shares the absence of resistance on the part of the scarecrow; the scarecrow is implicitly one with the wind. All of this is a powerful portrayal of wabi.

This autumn,
old age I feel
in the birds, the clouds.

The sabi quality of time passing. The birds and the clouds are passing, going away, leaving; autumn and old age resonate together.

Another, this one a haiku of Basho's in which both sabi and wabi are mixed.

I too
have no dwelling place
this autumn evening.

Basho was on a journey. The latter part of his life was spent traveling, and he died while on a trip. In this haiku he is traveling at night and sees the birds flying overhead and he says, "I too have no dwelling place this autumn evening." Traveling, particularly traveling in fifteenth-century Japan on horseback through wild and uncivilized country much of the time, never quite knowing where one was going to sleep, was the very essence of the sabi/wabi feeling. Furthermore, birds flying in autumn also evoke a feeling of loneliness, and the haiku gives very powerfully the poignant sense of the poverty and vast aloneness of autumn.

The last example is not about autumn but does illustrate so powerfully the feeling of sabi, melancholy loneliness. It was written by Issa. Issa was very poor. He had a family: a wife and two young daughters. First one of his daughters died; then his wife, and eventually his second daughter, who was still a baby, died. He wrote this haiku.

This is a dew drop world.
It may be a dew drop
and yet . . . and yet . . .

Many similarities exist between reading a haiku and working on a koan. When you read haiku—about the cold of autumn, homelessness, the dew drop—and evoke wabi and sabi, you must do so against the background of "no-self," epitomized by "No one walks along this path this autumn evening." If not, the tone degenerates into self-pity. It is the same when you work with a koan because, as has been said, you must work from an awakened mind.

This rather long preamble provides us an opportunity to appreciate an important twist in the koan. We cannot dwell for long with it, but the twist should nevertheless be pointed out.

The monk said to Chosha, "How much like the springtime you seem to be," and Chosha says, "It is better even than the autumn dews falling on the lotus leaves."

It can be said that springtime arouses the feeling of Oneness, of fullness. A master said, "The trees, the fields, the hills, the sky, these are my face." This is springtime. Autumn, on the other hand, is *emptiness*. "Vast emptiness and not a thing that can be called holy," in Bodhidharma's words. In the koan, the theme of Oneness and emptiness is present throughout: in going out through the fragrant grasses and coming back on the falling blossoms; in the fullness of springtime and the emptiness wabi/sabi of autumn. But why does Chosha say that one is better than the other, when they are both aspects of the same unity/emptiness? Both are exactly the same "thing" looked at from two different points of view. Why does Chosha say Oneness is better than emptiness; or does he really mean that?

It is like two lovers looking into each other's eyes.

COMMENTS ON THE VERSE

Let us now look at the verse, because it can help us see more clearly into this koan. *"The world without a speck of dust."* A master said, "From the beginning not a thing is." This is how we must see Chosha walking through the fields. Not a speck of dust anywhere. This is pure wabi, the ultimate of poverty. When it is said, "Blessed are the poor in spirit for theirs is the kingdom of heaven," it is saying that when one owns nothing, then one can own everything.

"Whose eyes are not opened?" Even dust is God's presence. Even the reflection is the mirror. The sound is the silence. Everything is the stillness. A disciple of a Hindu guru said, "Everything is an illusion." The guru said, "Do not insult Brahman." The reflection/mirror analogy breaks down at this point. Everything is just as it is. When we see it like that, where is there need for any discernment? We do not have to live our lives with the surgeon's scalpel constantly discerning one thing from another. You see it and then you go beyond it. This is awakening. "This earth where you stand is the pure Lotus Land; and this very body, the body of Buddha." No mirror, no reflection, just this earth where we stand, just this very body.

"First following the fragrant grasses, returning in pursuit of the falling blossoms." This is really just saying the same thing: the world without a speck of dust. This is pure openness, just cleanness. Broad daylight under a bright blue sky. And what is this openness, what is this emptiness, what is this mirror? *"First following the fragrant grasses, returning in pursuit of falling blossoms."* Everything manifests the way, everything is singing the songs of the dharma.

"The slender stork perched in the wintry tree." A classic sumi painting is of a shrike perched on a dead branch. This is wabi, this is sabi. But beyond it all there is just a slender stork

perched in the wintry tree. "*A crazed monkey shrieking on the age-old heights.*" When a loon cries out on a lake, the silence just shouts at you. It's like when you get just a single bird singing in the woods: the silence becomes palpable. It was said earlier that when you listen to the crickets, you are deafened by the silence.

> *With no bird singing,*
> *the mountain is yet more still.*

"A crazed monkey shrieking on the age-old heights. Chosha's eternal meaning." Chosha's eternal meaning. "Ah!"

_ . _ . _ . _ . _ . _ . _ . _ . _ . _ . _ . _ . _ . _ . _

> *Now we are saved absolutely, we need not say from*
> *what, we are at home in the universe and in principle*
> *and in the main, feeble and timid creatures as we are,*
> *there is nothing within the world or without it that can*
> *make us afraid.*

_ . _ . _ . _ . _ . _ . _ . _ . _ . _ . _ . _ . _ . _ . _

—Bosanquet

Rinzai Quote

Zen master Rinzai said:

Followers of the way, mind is without form and pervades the ten directions:

In the eye it is called seeing,
In the ear it is called hearing.
In the nose it smells odors,
In the mouth it holds converse.
In the hands it grasps and seizes,
In the feet it runs and carries.

Fundamentally, it is one pure radiance; divided, it becomes harmoniously united spheres of sense. Since the mind is nonexistent, wherever you go, you are free.

CHAPTER TWENTY-FOUR

Jewel Mirror Samadhi

The teaching of suchness has been intimately taught
by Buddhas and patriarchs:
now you have it, keep it well.
Filling a silver bowl with snow,
hiding a heron in the moonlight;
separate they are not the same
together they are not different.
The mind, free of words, responds to the slightest impulse;
if you're upset, it becomes a barrier;
if you miss it, you become anxious and full of doubts.
Neither dismiss nor confront
the great ball of fire.
To talk or write about it
is to defile it.
Bright at midnight;
it doesn't need the dawn to be seen.
It is the measure of all beings;
it is medicine for their suffering.
It does not act, but is not without words.
It is like gazing into a jewel mirror;
form and reflection know each other.
You are not it, but it is clearly you.
No going, no coming, no arising, no abiding.
In the end nothing is said, words are still not enough
because its speech is not yet correct.
Subtly included with the true,

question and answer come up together.

Innately pure yet inconceivable,

it is not within the realm of dream or awakening.

According to conditions, time and season,

quietly it shines.

Fine enough to penetrate where there is no space,

large enough to transcend all boundaries.

A hair's breadth and hell is heaven,

heaven is hell.

Now there are sudden and gradual,

because ways and means have been set up.

Once basic approaches are distinguished,

then there is right and wrong.

Outwardly calm while inwardly agitated,

like a tethered colt, a trapped rat:

The ancient saints pitied them,

and bestowed upon them the teaching;

in the midst of their confusion,

they called black as white.

Just let go of the confusion,

the mind will realize itself.

If you wish to conform to the ancient way,

please consider the ancients of former times:

Without fulfilling the way of Buddhahood,

Daitsu Chisho Buddha, spent ten kalpas beneath the tree of

contemplation.

For the benefit of those with inferior ability,

there are jewel footrests and brocaded robes;

for those capable of wonder, there is the lion and the white ox.

But when two arrows meet head on,

where can one find such skill?

When the wooden man begins to sing,

the stone maiden gets up to dance;

it's not grasped by the mind.

Why waste time reflecting upon it?

The servant obeys the Lord;

a son obeys the father.

It is unfilial not to obey, improper not to serve.
Practice secretly, working within,
appearing dull, seemingly stupid.
If you can persist in that,
this is called the host within the host.

The Stone Bridge of Joshu

THE CASE

A monk said to Joshu, "The stone bridge of Joshu is widely renowned, but coming here today, I find only a set of stepping stones." Joshu said, "You see only a set of stepping stones; you do not see the stone bridge."

"Well, what is the stone bridge?" the monk asked. Joshu said, "It lets asses cross and horses cross."

The Verse

> *No show of transcendence but his path was high.*
> *If you've entered the great sea of Zen, you should catch the*
> *giant turtle.*
> *One cannot help laughing at old Kankai, his contemporary,*
> *who said, "It is as quick as an arrow," a mere waste of time.*

Like all koans, this one too reveals true nature, but it also shows how true nature is revealed.

Before I comment on the koan itself, I would like to say something more about Joshu, because he and his teaching are not different; they are not two. Joshu was Joshu's teaching. This was possibly more true of him than of any other Zen master. Joshu was the essence of elegance, compassion, and gentleness; he was also right down to earth. He was a man who truly walked on his own feet.

He was awakened at the age of nineteen. It wasn't a great awakening by any means. He had a kensho when on asking Nansen, "What is the way?" Nansen replied, "Everyday mind is the way." Afterward he stayed with Nansen until Nansen's death, when Joshu was fifty-eight years of age. He then went on pilgrimage for about twenty years, visiting various teachers. Finally, at the age of eighty, he started teaching and continued to do so until the age of a hundred and thirty. Naturally, in all that time, many stories accumulated around him, and many of his sayings were recorded, some of which have already been given. However, I should like to tell one more.

A monk asked Joshu, "One who is completely without shame, where should one put him?" Joshu said, "Not here." The monk persisted, "But if such a one should show up, what would you do?" "I would boot him out."

Joshu implies that to claim one is devoid of shame is itself cause for shame. What does he mean by that? This koan is concerned with humility; it is through humility that true nature is ultimately revealed. *Shame* (perhaps a better word would be *remorse*) is the high road to humility. We must make a clear distinction between humility and humbleness. They have no connection at all; in fact, we may almost call them contraries. Humility always involves or implies dignity; the two go together. A person with true dignity is a person who has true humility. Shame is the process by which pride—dignity's shadow, the tendency we have to assert ourselves first and foremost—is undone. Shame is one of the virtues in Tibetan Buddhism. Hakuin speaks in an article that he wrote on practice about "shame driving us on."

A further distinction must be made between remorse and a tendency that many people have to criticize themselves, or to put themselves down. These people confess to all and sundry that they are no good. This is necessary because the crust, so to say, of ego has become so hard that remorse cannot flow in the way that it should. So, they have to resort simply to verbalizing their shame.

Another distinction still is between shame and being ashamed. Being ashamed is feeling shame in the presence of others. It is because of others that one is ashamed. One compares oneself adversely with others and, because of this comparison, one is ashamed. But the shame of which I am speaking is something like sorrow, it can come only with solitude.

All mondo (that is, question-and-answer between monks and masters) and all koans are ways by which we express the inexpressible, sometimes called the "no-self." It was this, probably more than anything else, that Buddha contributed to humankind; one could say that he drew attention to awakening. Shakyamuni would not have been the first to come to awakening. If he were, then awakening would not be part of the human situation, but instead something specific to certain kinds of people, and so dependent upon a particular form. This, of course, would be of no use to us. What we want above all is what does not come and go, what is not subject to birth and death, and so not dependent upon any kind of form. What we want is that which is immutable and totally, utterly, unequivocally reliable. Buddha drew attention to the importance of awakening to this immutability, awakening to it beyond all experience, beyond even the highest samadhi. The work of a Zen teacher is also to draw attention to this.

It has been said that simply hearing about awakening is of itself one of the most valuable things that can happen in life. Once you have heard, *truly heard,* about awakening, not simply read or heard the word "awakening" but assented to it in your inner heart as a consequence of hearing it, it becomes like a seed that has been fertilized and that in time is bound to grow. The time is painful, difficult, long, and weary, yes. But it is bound to grow. This is why Zen masters strive so hard to bring to people the message of awakening.

Let us return to the koan in which a monk said to Joshu, "The stone bridge of Joshu is widely renowned, but coming here today, I find only a set of stepping stones."

When working with a koan, you must always determine the degree of awakening of the protagonists. This determines how you will view the koan as a whole. In other words, how we are going to enter the koan. In this koan the monk is probably someone who has done very little work but is always prodding others to say something in the hope that they will do the work for him. Often such people ask very personal questions that they have no business asking but do so in the hope of getting a rise out of the person they are questioning, a reaction. They try to push him or her, but not in a constructive way.

This monk was saying to Joshu, "I've heard all about Joshu, but all I see is just a crummy little old man in front of me." In other words, "You look to me like a very ordinary person; what is so special about awakening?" *Joshu* was also the name of the town in which Joshu set up his teaching center. The town was built around one of the few bridges that crossed the wide rivers of China. It was therefore called the stone bridge of Joshu. It was not a bridge as we know it, but more like what we would call a ford, a series of stones that would enable one to cross. Because so few bridges or fords existed, it would have been widely known in China, particularly among travelers—and monks were inveterate travelers. So, most monks would have known about the stone bridge of Joshu. The monk stated, "The stone bridge of Joshu is widely renowned, but coming here today, I find only a set of stepping stones." And Joshu replied, "You see only a set of stepping stones; you do not see the stone bridge." What Joshu was saying is, what you see is what you get. You see only a set of stepping stones. However, this is not all he means. Zen master Dogen, when asked about what he had attained during the years he was in training in China, said, "I walk on my own feet; I see with my own eyes." Someone asked Joshu, "What is right before one's eyes?" Joshu said, "You are what is right before one's eyes."

Setcho's verse says, "One cannot help laughing at old Kankai . . . who said, 'It is as quick as an arrow,' a mere waste of time." What Setcho was referring to in his verse is a mondo very similar in meaning to the koan with which we are dealing: "A monk came to see Kankai and said, 'Kankai is widely renowned [in this case Kankai was a great lake] but coming here I find only a puddle.' " And Kankai said much the same as Joshu; he said, "You see only a puddle and do not see Kankai." But then the monk asked, "What is Kankai?" And Kankai said, "It is as quick as an arrow." Setcho is saying that the last remark of Kankai's spoiled it—it was too much. He shouldn't have gone on to say "It is as quick as an arrow." This is why Setcho says that one has to laugh at old Kankai.

When Tokusan went to see Ryutan, he said, "Ryutan is well known, but now I am here, I see neither dragon [*ryu*] nor abyss [*tan*]." What he was saying is, I've heard about this dragon-abyss, Ryutan, but now, I'm here and find neither dragon nor abyss. And Ryutan said, "You see Ryutan with your very eyes." Seeing is enough. People look for miracles, overlooking the miracle of seeing. Layman P'ang, a famous layman in China, said, "My miraculous activity and magical power, drawing water and chopping wood."

Push aside what you see, and then what do you see? Let go of what it is that you know, and then what do you know? Somebody who went to Nisargadatta said, "As I look at you, you seem to be a poor man with very limited means, facing all the problems of poverty and old age just like everyone else." Nisargadatta said, "I am neither rich nor poor." If he is neither rich nor poor, what is he? Furthermore, if he is neither rich nor poor, how can one know Nisargadatta?

Rinzai's teaching was of the man of no rank, the person that is poor in spirit. China was a very hierarchic society: everyone had a rank. A man of no rank just did not exist. It was like the military hierarchy of today: second lieutenant, first lieutenant, captain, major, lieutenant-colonel, colonel, and all the rest of it, then down through sergeant major, sergeant, corporal first class and second class, and so on. Everyone in the army has a rank. But Rinzai spoke of the man of *no rank*. Imagine someone in the army who has no rank. The person of no rank is the One. Rinzai's teaching is "As I see it, there is not much to do, just be ordinary." Just be ordinary. And this is what this koan is about. Just be ordinary, a man of no rank.

T. S. Eliot says, "Humility is endless." What does it mean? It means one no longer appropriates everything to oneself, no longer takes everything that happens as it affects "me." Everyone knows what they were doing when Kennedy was shot. Everyone knows because everyone related it immediately to their own situation. It reminds me of the bumper sticker of the sixties, "An atomic war could ruin your whole day." We have this tendency, no matter what happens, to refer it back to ourselves, back to "I." How will I be affected by this? We do this because I am the One and I seek to reflect wholeness in terms of the "I," in terms of being the center. Mircea Eliade the mythologist said, "The search to be at the center is the nostalgia for paradise. By this we mean to find oneself always and without effort in the center of the world, at the heart of reality. And by a short cut, and in a natural manner, to transcend the human condition and to recover the divine condition or, as the Christians would say, the condition before the fall." The condition before the fall; this is what we seek. And we seek it by seeking to be at the center; this is the nostalgia for paradise. Always and without effort to be in the center of the world, at the heart of reality. And by a short cut, and in a natural manner, to transcend the human condition.

How many people practice Zen in order, "by a short cut, and in a natural manner, to transcend the human condition." One could say that "I," the need to be at the center, the need to transcend the human condition and to be the one, is the cause of all our anxieties. In the end, the only true cure for our anxieties is humility. Again let me repeat, I do not mean self-castigation, being ashamed or humble. I do not mean walking around with a bent back. The way to humility is to allow this feeling of remorse to permeate, to be present in one's practice. It may manifest itself as a very deep sadness. Someone pointed out to me that people aren't sad these days, because sadness is essentially solitary. We're depressed or anxious or put out or down or flat, but the idea of sadness seems to have lost its hold on the feeling equipment, so to say, of human beings.

"Identity, individuality, uniqueness," as one teacher said, "are the most valuable aspects of the mind, yet of the mind only. 'I am all there is,' also is an experience equally valid. They are two aspects of the nameless." To know the nameless, one must let go of this *demand* to be the unique center. This does not mean that one lets go of the center. No, as this teacher said, "Identity, individuality, uniqueness, they are the most valuable aspects of the mind." This is how the mind operates. It's not that we have to destroy them; we must fulfill them. To let go of the demon, the desire to be the One, is to fulfill oneself as an individual. Letting go is not falling into an abyss but opening up into the light. But again, we're faced with the dilemma that yawns constantly in the very heart of the human being, the blessed wound.

It is said that in the Greek sense of tragedy, a person's unique excellence (which is *arate*) is identical with his tragic flaw (which is *hamasha*). This is like the nun who said, "I cannot pull up the weed (hamasha) because if I do, I shall pull up the flower (arate)." Center and unity, "I" and wholeness, self and Self, these are not two, but they are not the same either. This is why, although the truth is fundamentally simple and before our very eyes, it takes so long for us to realize it. It is not that we should do things differently. This also is too simplistic. Nor is it a question of "giving things up." Many people feel that the spiritual path is to give up possessions or to cut down on eating food or to give up friendship and friendly relations with people, and so on. To give up. This is too simplistic. Anyone can give things up. We're not even talking about giving up egotism or ambition. What we're suggesting is that one comes to see it within a wider framework. It is like what Shunryu Suzuki said, "If you want to control a bull, put it in a big field." This is to say that the demand to be the only one, to be special, important, is seen against the background of wholeness, and when this happens we feel shame.

Joshu said, "You see only a set of stepping stones; you do not see the stone bridge." And then the monk went on and said, "Well, what is the stone bridge?" And then Joshu said, "It lets asses cross and horses cross." Joshu is talking about what, in his day, would have been an ordinary, everyday occurrence. People would be on a journey with their horses and their asses, and they would cross this bridge.

But the stone bridge could do no more than the set of stepping stones could do. So, why is this distinction made between a bridge and stepping stones? Why on the one hand talk about a stone bridge and on the other about stepping stones? It is like talk about Self and self, why make the distinction?

To answer this we must go back to what we said at the very beginning of this talk: Joshu's teaching is Joshu. Eventually, we must come to see the world just as it is. There is no Buddha-nature, no real self, no mind, no light of the world, no wholeness, no awakening. All these are but props, ways of talking. In other words, what we do, eventually, is come back to the stepping stones. But these stepping stones are the stone bridge; the stone bridge is these stepping stones. But we're not talking about "is" and "are" of identity. We're not saying form is *identical* to emptiness, that emptiness is *identical* to form. If we were to do that, then we turn the whole thing into a farcical tautology. It is not the one of identity, but neither is it two: form on the one hand and emptiness on the other; self on the one hand and Self on the other. We are now talking about what has no roots; Oneness and twoness, identity and difference, are roots. How do you give expression to that with no roots? Someone asked this of Joshu, who said, "But are you not expressing yourself at this very moment?"

Setcho's verse says, "No show of transcendence but his path was high."

No show of transcendence. This is the mark of a mature teacher, a mature spiritual person. When one first comes to awakening, one has got something. One feels that one has somehow "made it." But after a while, after one sees more deeply, one realizes that much work has to be done. In life to be able "to suffer the slings and arrows of outrageous fortune," one often has to build bunkers of concrete, reinforced concrete and very thick. One kensho, even a deep one, rarely breaks down these bunkers. After the Second World War, I was employed in the East End of London, during holidays while at school, to break down air-raid shelters that had been built of solid reinforced concrete. In those days the equipment was still quite primitive in comparison with what is available now, and so most of the work was done with just sheer effort using sledgehammers and chisels. That is Zen practice: sledgehammers and chisels. It was also extremely dry, dusty work. Because we were digging out bunkers that had been air-raid shelters, the work was very often in a very dim kind of light. It was endless; the work just went on and on. But at least we knew the air-raid shelters were no longer necessary, and so we did the work with an attitude of great liberation, of great freedom. These air-raid shelters were just so much rocks, so much concrete. And after kensho more and more this is how one sees one's defenses, one's attitudes and opinions—they are so much rock, so much concrete. One must not expect them to vanish overnight. On the contrary, I know only too well, it takes years and years.

This koan is utter simplicity. When one first reads it, one wonders, What is there in it?

A monk said to Joshu, "The stone bridge of Joshu is widely renowned, but coming here today, I find only a set of stepping stones." Joshu said, "You see only a set of stepping stones; you do not see the stone bridge."

"What is the stone bridge?" the monk asked. Joshu said, "It lets asses cross and horses cross."

It is bare. There is nothing to it and yet, just as there is also nothing to Joshu, just a little old man, it contains everything, everything!

As T. S. Eliot says, "Humility is endless."

—·—·—·—·—·—·—·—·—·—·—·—·—·—

For, and St. Bernard is my witness,
"Perfect humility knows no bounds."

—·—·—·—·—·—·—·—·—·—·—·—·—·—

—Cloud of Unknowing

Quotes from Joshu

Someone asked, "What is my essence?"

Joshu said, "The tree moves in the wind, the bird flies above, the fish leaps, the water is muddy."

A monk asked, "It is said, 'It is empty, it is clear, it shines of itself.' To shine of itself, what does it mean?"

Joshu replied, "It does not mean that something else shines."
The monk went on, "When it fails to shine, what then?"
"You have betrayed yourself."

A monk asked, "Where is that which is neither day nor night?"
Joshu replied, "Now is it day? Now is it night?"
My question is not about now.
You cannot do away with me.

"True teaching is without form. But with no master and no pupil, how is it then?"
Joshu said, "Who made you ask this question?"
"No one in particular."
Joshu hit him.

The one who is beyond good and evil, does he obtain deliverance?
He does not.

Why not?
Because he is within good and evil.

What is the principal concern of the one wearing the Buddhist robes?
Not to deceive himself.

One who is entirely devoid of shame, where should one put him?
Not here.
If such a one should show up, what would you do?
Kick him out.

What is right before one's eyes?
You are what is right before one's eyes.

Someone asked, "What is the one word?"
What are you saying?

Joshu said, "When I am hungry, I eat; when I am tired, I sleep."

A monk asked, "What is Buddha?"
Joshu replied, "The oak tree in the garden."

Someone asked Joshu, "What about the cold spring of the ancient brook?"
"It tastes bitter."
"What happens to the drinker?"
"He dies."

One morning as Joshu was greeting new arrivals to his monastery, he asked one, "Have you been here before?" "No," replied the newcomer. "Have a cup of tea," said Joshu. Another monk came, and Joshu asked him the same question. "Yes," replied the monk. "Have a cup of tea." The head monk remonstrated with Joshu, saying, "The one who had not been here before you gave a cup of tea, to the one who had been here before you gave a cup of tea. What are you up to?" "Have a cup of tea."

"I have nothing," said a monk. "Then put it down," said Joshu. "How can I put it down?" "Then carry it away."

"What is your understanding?" "I have nothing inside, and I seek for nothing outside."

"Who is Buddha?" "Who are you?"

"What is the most fundamental teaching?" "You must excuse me, I must have a piss. Think, even such a trifling thing I have to do it myself."

CHAPTER TWENTY-SEVEN

On Death

A Zen master asked, "If you realize your true nature, you are free from life and death. Tell me, when your eyesight dims in the final moments, how can you be free from life and death?" He then went further, asking, "When you free yourself from life and death, you should know where you are going. So, when the four elements disintegrate, where will you go?"

The master was calling upon us to come face to face with death, something that most of us are reluctant to do. No one needs to be told that the question of death has haunted us ever since humankind has been on earth. The Gilgamesh epic, written about four or five thousand years ago, is the story of Gilgamesh, who is hunting for a resolution of what it means to die. On one occasion, after the death of his friend Enkidu, he calls out, "Me! Will I too not die like Enkidu? Sorrow has come to my belly. I fear death."[1]

What is death? The same question was raised in the Vedic hymns, the Upanishads; throughout Greece; through the Hebrew tradition; in the Sufi tradition; and so on. It is a fundamental question. Various alternative solutions have been given. In general, the religious reactions to it can be divided into two broad categories: those that give solace and reassurance and that seek to give us comfort in the face of the fact of death, and those, much rarer, that aim at stripping away all comfort, all myths and beliefs, to push us to face the truth. And the truth is far more glorious than any heaven that the myths can possibly imagine. Most mythical afterlives, if one follows them through logically, end up with infinite boredom.

When you truly think about death, it can bring up the deepest anguish and despair. Ask yourself, "Where will I be in a hundred years' time? In two hundred years' time, what will have happened?" I do not know the given names of my grandparents, and as far as my great-grandparents are concerned, I've got no idea who they were, where they lived, or what they did for a living. Yet they must have died a mere one hundred years ago. Even so, I know nothing about them. As for their parents, anything concerning them is lost in the never-never land of nowhere! So in a hundred years' time what about you? In two hundred years the world will be populated by total strangers who quite likely will have different values, different languages, different nations, and different lifestyles. You and I will have vanished like snowflakes fallen on a hot stove. Not only you and I, but everyone we meet, work with, live with, love, and hate. When we truly contemplate this (and the worst time to do it is at two-thirty, one sleepless night), a dark dread invades us. What does it all mean? How many poets have asked this overwhelming question?

I remember Shakespeare talked about death being "that undiscover'd country from whose bourn no traveller returns." An undiscovered country. . . . He said, "To die, to sleep. To sleep, perchance to dream. Ay! There's the rub. For in that deep sleep of death, what dreams may come when we've shuffled off this mortal coil?"

The fear of death, the fear of something after death, and—the biggest fear of all—the fear of nothing after death were, after all, what drove Buddha into the forest to search for awakening. We can say that he was inspired by the love of humankind, that he came down from the highest Tushita heaven, that he wanted to find a way to alleviate the suffering of all humanity. But it is much more likely that he was like you and me: tormented, uncertain, longing to know, having to find something ultimate. Tradition says he met a sick man, an old man, and a dead man. Each one of us has met those in our day.

206

Not necessarily a physical meeting, but in our hearts when we wonder and worry, "What does it mean? What is it all about?"

When we think and worry about death, we think about a whole complex that is all jumbled up. Furthermore, because so often the whole idea of it is so fearful, we never have the courage to sort it out, to untangle this complexity we call death.

If, for a moment, we can think about it now, what comes to us most easily is the death of "them," of "those," "the others." This is the statistical death, the death that we can count and philosophize about; we can talk about how serious it is—in Bosnia, Africa, or Russia. We can sympathize and want to organize aid, write to our MPs or representatives about it, be charitable, and so on. But it's all impersonal. These days, because of television, we can even sometimes get confused as to whether a death is real or whether it is just another bottle of tomato ketchup that's being spilled. Death as well as evil has become banal. The impersonal death is very often the kind of death that people think about when they say, "I'm not afraid of death." It is the death of "them," the faceless multitude; and they see themselves as part of that multitude.

But then I encounter the death of someone whom I love. This is a different death; it calls for a different kind of confrontation. No longer is it impersonal, something that I can hold at arm's length; indeed, it is so personal that it goes beyond the person: it is not only a death of a person, it is also the ripping, tearing away of part of my life, part of my world. We have to reevaluate our whole life to rediscover a new meaning when someone very close dies. Nothing is the same; everything has to be reexamined. We have to let go of "someone," but this someone is the nexus of memories, a storehouse of love and regret, laughter and guilt, joy and jangling times of mutual misunderstandings, and, yes, hatred. Our life has to be put into new order. This is very painful, as all kinds of mixed emotions arise because of all the relationships that have been destroyed and lost forever. A man was trying to console a friend whose wife had just died, saying not to weep so much, because it would not help the situation, And the friend said, "Yes, and that is why I weep."

When we meet this kind of death, we must know how to mourn. But because in our modern society we are overwhelmed by impersonal death, because we cannot easily make a distinction between it and the fracturing of a world, we have forgotten how to mourn. We pretend that this death too is just something else that has happened in our lives, another experience, "something we can learn from" rather than a fundamental change in our whole life.

It probably takes two or three years of mourning fully to work through the death of someone close to us. We have to face the death daily but more intensely at those special times of the year such as birthdays, Christmas, times by the lake, times when we need a friend to turn to and talk with. Yet, if we know how to mourn, the process is a healing one, healing in a way that is difficult to describe but directly known and realized. Furthermore, the mourning can bring the loved one's life also to a completion and a fulfillment.

At the end of a sesshin, I often say to people, "Be careful about two or three days after sesshin, you're likely to go into a period of mourning; you're likely to get a feeling of the blues." The reason for this admonition is that during a sesshin, we lose certain values—illusory ones, it is true, but values nevertheless. Because of this the "I" loses its central position; it has, in a certain measure, died. So we must go through this reevaluation, not necessarily at a conscious level—in fact, most often it is at what is erroneously called the "unconscious" level, a level that is really the true conscious level. The healing process, that is, the process of becoming whole again, after a sesshin and after the death of a loved one, is not different in kind, although very different in degree. But the first can prepare us for the second.

Even during the practice of zazen itself, we pass through periods of mourning that often take the form of deep remorse, deep sadness. This deep sadness is fundamental to the religious experience and was captured for all time in Michelangelo's *Pieta*. The Arabic word *allah* comes from a root word meaning "sadness." Gurdjieff used to talk about "our all-suffering Creator." This sadness comes when the gulf between "I" and "thou" dissolves and I see myself as you see me when you are no longer there to see me.

But a third death must yet be faced, and this is the death that each one of us must die. It is this death that the master wants us to confront. He says quite specifically, "If you realize your true nature, you're free from life and death. Tell me, when your eyesight dims in the final moments, how can you be free from life and death?" And then, "When you free yourself from life and death, you should know where you're going. So, when the four elements disintegrate, where will you go?"

Now and again people ask me to recommend books about death, because they would like to read about death and so prepare themselves for it. But no book can prepare us for our own death. We cannot learn about this death from the outside. We can see a hundred or a thousand people die; we can have every close member of the family around us die, but we still know nothing about our own death. We know what death is like from the outside, we know how "they" die; we also know the different kinds of agonies that death can induce and the different kinds of difficulties that people have. But this is death from the outside, and our own death is essentially death from inside. The only way in which we can learn about our own death is by dying. And truly, this is what our practice is about. There used to be some Irish monks who would meditate in their coffins. The Carmelite nuns also would dig a spade full of earth from their grave each day. True religious practice is the practice of dying. In the seventeenth century a practice of meditation swept across Europe, and one of the primary subjects for meditation was death. Christ says, "Truly I say unto you, unless a grain of wheat falls into the earth and dies, it remains alone. But if it dies, it bears much fruit."

It is this kind of death that we are talking about—the grain of wheat that must die. Angelus Silesius once said, "If you die before you die, you do not die when you die."

People say that you do not know what happens when you die, and this is quite true. Someone asked Hakuin, "What happens when one dies?" and Hakuin said, "I do not know!" And the questioner said, "You do not know! Aren't you a Zen master?"

Hakuin said, "Sure, I'm a Zen master, but not a dead one."
While it is true that we do not know what happens after death,
it is also true that we do not know what will happen tomorrow.
Yet, someone might say, we can nevertheless be fairly certain we
shall be around tomorrow. But then what about sleep? We do
not know what happens when we sleep, can we even say we are
around when we sleep? What does one mean when one looks
ahead and feels certain that one "will be around"?

If we look at our lives, as we so often do, from the outside, if we look at them simply as mechanical actions that we
have to perform reluctantly, unwillingly, but necessarily,
because we have to feed and clothe ourselves, then we do not
even know what is happening right now. Moment by moment
goes by in a state of almost total unawareness. You must have
passed through days yourself when you were "asleep" all day. In
retrospect, it seems as though that day were a dream, as much a
dream as the dream we dream at night.

Yet, even at such a time, awareness formed the background of each moment. Likewise, awareness is present as a
background even during the night, but one does not remember.
It is memory that enables us to say, "Yes, I was aware, I was
conscious." But even without memory, awareness is not absent.
When I say I do not know what will happen to me tomorrow,
but at least I shall be around, I mean at least awareness will be
present. Buddha says that the most wonderful thing is that
everyone sees people dying around them but is unable to con-
ceive of their own death. This is true because we cannot con-
ceive of ourselves as not being. Even our fear of annihilation is
a fear of being aware in total darkness and silence.

Even though most of us are unable to consider our own
death, if we could do so, we would most likely consider it in a
confused way. We worry about the actual process of dying, the
pain of it, the indignity of it. Mixed in with this is the sorrow at
leaving life and all whom we love, at leaving the beauty of
spring, the languidness of summer, the melancholy of autumn,
and the austerity of winter. But underlying this, and reinforcing
the fear and the pain, is a much deeper fear, a metaphysical
fear, a fear of the loss of self.

Someone said to a Zen master, "I'm not afraid of death," and the Zen master said, "Oh! What a pity!" A writer who was much more in touch with himself said, "We are the fools of time and terror. Days steal on us and steal from us. Yet we live, loathing our life and yet dreading still to die." Dreading still to die is the metaphysical fear of death; this is the fear we have to work with when doing zazen.

We often ask students this question: "What is it that you can take with you? When the doctor does one day say, 'I've got some bad news for you,' then what? What is it that you'll take across that line?" The reason for this question is not to induce morbid thoughts but that, if you seriously ask it, you are going to have to sift the coarse from the fine. You are going to have to work with discernment. Perhaps the question would be more accurately asked, "What survives death?" because of course "you" are one of the things left behind. But to ask the question about survival makes it abstract. "What will you take with you?" makes it more immediate, more dramatic.

We do not know how we're going to die. The question is not asked to prepare us to have a good, heroic, or stoic death. Each of us will die according to the circumstances in which we find ourselves at the time. If we're fortunate, we'll have a peaceful death; but it may be that we'll have a tormented death. It may be that we will have to go through a lot of pain and anguish in the process of dying. But the value of looking into this question of "What is it that you are going to take across the line?" is not in preparing you for the actual physical fact of the death process, but so that you can die *now* the metaphysical death. The question, if asked seriously, makes you let go of those things that you know you cannot take across the line; as has just been said, this includes "you." In turn, you see into what it is that you truly are.

Nisargadatta says,

To be a living being is not the ultimate state. There is something beyond, much more wonderful, which is neither being nor non-being; neither living nor not living. It is a state of pure awareness, beyond the limitation of space and time. Once the illusion that the body/mind of oneself is abandoned, death loses its terror. It becomes part of living.

In saying this he is, probably without knowing it, echoing Buddha, "There is that sphere wherein is neither earth nor water, fire nor air: it is not the infinity of space, nor the infinity of perception; it is not nothingness, nor is it neither idea nor nonidea; it is neither this world nor the next, nor is it both; it is neither the sun nor the moon. It neither comes nor goes, it neither abides nor passes away; it is not caused, established, begun, supported; it is the end of suffering."

To awaken to pure awareness is to die to the awareness of "I am a human being," or "I am something." In the same way to die to pure awareness is to awaken to "I am a human being." To come home to ourselves as pure awareness means that we have let go of all the thoughts, ideas, memories, and constructs that we have about ourselves. But essentially, it means that we have let go of the idea of "I," "*I* am something separate," "*I* am a unique, separate, individual, isolated, special being." The Christians call this insistence upon "I," pride.

We have a sense of being a solid something, although if put to the test, we are totally unable to say what we mean by this. My own reaction when I first heard Yasutani-roshi say that the "I" was an illusion was to dismiss what he was saying as another of those clever Zen things. It was some time before I could accept that he meant it literally, and even longer still before I got a faint whiff of what he really meant. It is for this illusory something that the myths find an afterlife and that people believe is going to survive death. An important aspect of the illusory something for modern human beings is the personality. For most of us, the personality has taken the place once occupied by the soul. Above all, we feel, it must be this personality that is going to survive death, this bundle of loves and hates, judgments, opinions, hopes, and fears that, we hope, will somehow survive; all of this seems our treasure.

But this personality is changing constantly. Have you noticed that you do not have one "I" but many? You have an "I" with its behavior patterns when you are with your spouse, another when you are with your parent, another when you are with your child, another when you are with your boss, and so on. Which "I" are you going to take across with you? Which "I" is going to undertake this journey? Is it the "I" that you are when you're at work with your colleagues? The "I" that you are when you are in bed with your spouse or lover? Is it the "I" that you are secretly when you're whimpering under the blows and curses of life in the early hours of the morning? Which "I" is it you're going to take? All of them? Is it going to be the "I" that you were when you were a two-year-old child? The "I" that you are when you're in hospital dying? One of the interesting phenomena that have turned up in modern psychology is what is called the multiple personality, in which there are literally a number of "I"s, sometimes up to a hundred, inhabiting one body. Most of these "I"s invariably know nothing about the others. Some of them speak different languages; one might like one kind of cigarette, another a different kind, and a third doesn't smoke. Some have illnesses that the others do not. In a man there are sometimes female "I"s, and in women, male "I"s.

Billy Milligan was a multiple personality who turned out to be a rapist. But the rapist was a lesbian female "I" who inhabited his body. In a multiple personality, a central coordinating principle has not been able to withstand the suffering that was inflicted on it very early on, and so multiple principles are generated. Thus, no central coordinating factor develops; instead a succession of them sprout up, each with its own memories, ideas, and so on. A "normal" person could be likened to a tree with a single trunk; a multiple personality would be like a series of shoots. Nevertheless, in that the tree has a number of branches, we are all in a way multiple personalities. Which one is going to heaven? It is not surprising that many people, including psychologists who have been called upon to treat multiple personalities, have rejected the whole idea—some saying that it is just an act being put on to avoid taking responsibility for actions. To accept the idea of multiple personalities throws into question what it means to be an individual.

One of the ways to handle multiple personalities is to let

each one slowly merge with a dominant central personality. However, when a personality hears that it is going to be merged, it is sometimes very afraid—it believes it is going to die. One case on record tells of a woman whose personalities were being merged by the therapist. One of them, however, refused to be merged until the therapist had spoken to a priest and had received from him assurance that the merging would not in any way damage the soul of that personality.

Which one is going to survive death? When one looks at it like this, when one really considers it like this, then one can see that the idea of individual survival, this idea that we go from body to body as individuals or that we go to some heaven as individuals, is just a myth. I was talking about this the other day to someone who said, "Thank goodness it is a myth! Who would want to see survive this personality, with all of its contradictions, hates, petty jealousies, and tormented sense of its own importance?" Whoever has done some work on themselves during a sesshin would surely say amen to that.

This is the illusion: that we are *something,* that we are an immortal, eternal "I." To wake up is to wake up to the source from which "I" gets its animation and power. The "I" is not some disincarnate ghost in the body. The "I" and the body are one, but they are not the same. We talk about the body/mind and perhaps we should talk about the body/minds in the plural. But what is it that animates the body? What is it that animates the mind? We sometimes ask people who come for private interview, "Who came through the door?" or "Who rang the bell?" In other words, what animates this body? Modern science, with all the power of its technology and marvelous subtle reasoning, cannot help us in the least. This is because modern science can know only *things,* and even then only know the surfaces of things, or more precisely yet, the relationship between things; and these things in turn are but a set of relationships. And you are not a thing, you are not a relation.

So, where can we look for this question of what is death; how do I die my death? Another question that we sometimes ask is "What happens to a thought when it is no longer being thought? Where does it go?" It is a good question to ask yourself. It's very much like another one, "What happens to the light of a candle when the light is blown out?" On the superficial level, it seems to be a ridiculous question. But really, what one is asking at the same time is, Where does that light come from? Where does that thought come from? Where the thought goes to and where the thought comes from are not two different places. And where does light get its light from? Where does the sun get its light from?

Buddha asks, "If the bell stops ringing, do you stop hearing?" If there is nothing to see, do you stop seeing? This question is the same as "What is the sound of one hand clapping?" At what time would one have the ultimate nothing to see, nothing to hear? Of course, the answer is death. If you can see into the sound of one hand clapping, you have seen into life and death. The Surangama Sutra says, "Even in dreams, when all thinking has become quiescent, the hearing nature is still alert. It is like a mirror to awakening that is transcendental to the thinking mind because it is beyond the consciousness sphere of both body and mind."

It is said if Buddha is in life and death, there is no life and death. Buddha is the sound of one hand clapping, the face before your parents were born, your true nature. And as Tosotsu says, "If you see into your true nature, if you realize your true nature, you are free from life and death."

Tosotsu goes on and asks, "When you free yourself from life and death, you should know where you're going. So when the four elements disintegrate, where will you go?" Someone asked this question of Ramana Maharshi, the great Hindu saint, when he was dying. And Ramana Maharshi said, "I'm not going anywhere, there's nowhere to go." Another master said, "My body is so big, there is nowhere to put it." Yet another said, "The mountains, trees, fields, rivers, these are my face. The sound of the birds and the sound of the wind is my voice." Where can the master go?

This question that the master asks, which we have changed to "What can you take across the line?," is possibly the most penetrating of all questions. If one is serious in one's practice, it is a question that must occur again and again. It's the sort of question that is the basis of the practice. Do not waste your time looking for consolation. Consolation is simply another set of thoughts, another set of ideas. To really work on yourself means that you are going to take everything that comes and see it as something that has come from outside you, as something other than you and so, therefore, can be let go of. Everything that you have ever thought or heard or feared about death is something that has come from outside you. And so, therefore, you can let it go too.

—·—·—·—·—·—·—·—·—·—·—·—·—·—·—·—

*The sole means now for saving the unfortunate beings
of earth [would be to ensure] that everyone of these
unfortunates during the process of existence should constantly sense and be cognizant of his own death as well
as the death of everyone upon whom his eyes or attention rests.*

—·—·—·—·—·—·—·—·—·—·—·—·—·—·—·—

—Gurdjieff

The Diamond Sutra: "The Transgression Is Wiped"

The Diamond Sutra says, "If a virtuous man or woman receives, holds in mind, reads, and recites this sutra and is scornfully reviled by others, this person has done wicked deeds in previous ages; because of this he or she falls onto hard times. Nevertheless, because of this scorn and vilification in this life, the wicked action of the former ages is thereby exhausted."

KOANS BRING US TO AWAKENING, NOT CONCERNED WITH MORALITY

This koan is quite unusual. Each koan must, in its resolution, bring us to awakening; it does not simply transform our understanding. We do not acquire a greater insight or develop a more harmonious understanding of existence, the resolution of a koan is the resolution of our life, our life situation. Furthermore, koans do not give us a moral code by which to live. They are not concerned with making us better people. In Zen it is said that one must cut the root. Devoting one's energies and attention to being a better person falls into the realm of pruning the weed, cutting it back. If one cuts the root, then the leaves and the branches, the flower, the fruit, are all taken care of. Now the question is, In what way does this koan allow us to cut the root?

At first glance the koan seems to be preaching a form of fundamentalism. It seems to be saying that the sutra has a magical property and that just holding it, or reciting from it, has healing efficacy. Indeed, at the time that this koan collection was compiled, many people interpreted the sutra in just this way. One preacher, for example, built a case to hold the Tripitika and that could be turned so that passages could be read at random. While this "turning" was going on, memorized passages of the scripture would be recited; and in this way one would gain merit from the sutras.

One cannot think of anything that would be further from the spirit of Bodhidharma, who taught "a special tradition outside the scriptures with no dependence upon words and letters." But if the sutra is not teaching some form of fundamentalism, what is it teaching? To be able to answer this, we must know more about the Diamond Sutra. A Zen monk or nun of the tenth century tackling this koan would have known this sutra very well and would have had no need for a commentary on it; but we, in our day, do not have this familiarity. However, the koan is pushing us onto the teaching of the Diamond Sutra, as this will make sense of the rest of the koan. So when you read the following about the Diamond Sutra, you must read more than the words. You must "read" yourself as well.

COMMENTS UPON THE DIAMOND SUTRA

The sixth Zen patriarch, Hui-neng, came to awakening after he heard an itinerant monk recite from the Diamond Sutra, "Arouse the mind without resting it on anything." Later, when the fifth patriarch was giving transmission of the robe and bowl to Hui-neng, he also expounded the Diamond Sutra. When he came to the passage, "Arouse the mind without resting it on anything," Hui-neng underwent a further deep awakening.

Zen tradition insists upon Hui-neng's illiteracy and poverty and on his being a layman at the time of his awakening. This means, in effect, that it is possible for all to come to awakening, no matter how poor, how uneducated, or what status he or she has in the social stratum, or even whether he or she has heard of Buddhism. This is the message of Hui-neng. That he was a layman is also important. In Zen practice, emphasis was put on the equality of lay and ordained practice. Putting all this in a nutshell, awakening is not dependent upon any kind of status, system, or training; *it is intrinsic to human nature.* This too is the teaching of the Diamond Sutra.

ORDINARINESS OF BUDDHA

The opening paragraph of the sutra, which sets the stage for all that follows, shows that the teaching is ordinary, down-to-earth. "One day at breakfast time the World-Honored One put on his robe and, carrying his bowl, made his way into the great city of Shravasti to beg for his food. In the midst of the city, he begged from door to door according to the rule. This done, he returned to his retreat and ate his meal. When he had finished, he put away his robe and begging bowl, washed his feet, arranged his seat, and sat down."

What is remarkable about that passage is how unremarkable it is. This is just an ordinary monk, doing the things that a monk does. An old man begs for his food according to the rules of the order, eats it, washes his feet, and sits down. How different the passage is from one taken, say, from the Avatamsaka:

> As soon as the Buddha had entered this concentration, the magnificent pavilion became boundlessly vast, the surface of the earth appeared to be made of indestructible diamond, the surface of the ground covered with a net of all the finest jewels strewn around with flowers of many jewels with enormous gems strewn all over; it was adorned with sapphire pillars with well-proportioned decorations of world-illuminating pearls of the finest water, with all kind of gems combined in pairs adorned with heaps of gold, and jewels with a dazzling array of turrets, arches, chambers, windows, and balconies.

Later on in the Diamond Sutra Buddha asks his disciple, Subhuti, "Is the Tathagata to be recognized by some material characteristic?" and Subhuti replies, "No, World-Honored One; the Tathagata cannot be recognized by any material characteristic." It was generally believed that the Buddha could be recognized by his having thirty-two distinguishing characteristics or marks. The question could equally have been rendered as "Can

Buddha be recognized by any kind of behavior, by anything he is, does, or says?" Subhuti answers, "No, World-Honored One, the Tathagata cannot be recognized by any material characteristic." This can be interpreted in two ways: what is essentially Buddha is beyond all form, or that Buddha himself is an ordinary person, nothing distinguishes him in appearance from anyone else.

TEACHING OF THE DIAMOND SUTRA: NO TEACHING, NO ATTAINMENT

In another excerpt Subhuti asks, "World-Honored One, if good men and good women wish to come to deep awakening, what rule of conduct should they have and how should they control their thoughts?" Subhuti, in other words, is asking for Buddha's teaching. And Buddha says, "I will declare to you what the rule of conduct is." "I will teach you."

This, then, is how the Diamond Sutra begins, with Subhuti asking for teaching on behalf of good men and good women, and Buddha promising to give it. Yet, later on, Buddha asks, "Has the Tathagata a teaching to enunciate?" (Now, don't forget earlier Buddha has undertaken to teach.) And Subhuti answers, "As I understand Buddha's meaning, there is no formulation of truth called complete awakening. . . . Moreover, the Tathagata has no formulated teaching to enunciate. Why? Because Tathagata has said that truth is uncontainable and inexpressible. It neither is nor is not." There is no complete awakening, formulation of truth; nor is there any teaching.

That is one of the most important phrases or paragraphs in the Diamond Sutra: no attainment, no incomparable awakening to attain no teaching; and no way that is taught. What is this "no teaching"? It is obviously not an absence of teaching!

NO BEING TO LIBERATE

In another important paragraph that has a bearing on our koan, Buddha says, "Bodhisattvas, all people who are practicing the way with any kind of diligence, should discipline their thoughts thus: 'All living beings are caused by me to attain Unbounded

Liberation Nirvana. Yet, when an uncountable, immeasurable number of beings have been liberated, *no being has been liberated.*' Why is this? It is because no bodhisattva who is a real bodhisattva cherishes the idea of an ego-entity, a personality, a being or a separated individuality." Anatman, no-ego-entity, is a fundamental teaching of Buddhism. Just as "no teaching" does not mean the absence of teaching, so "no-self" does not mean the absence of self. In his *Verses in Praise of Zazen,* Hakuin Zenji says that we should turn inward and "prove our true nature, that true self is no-self, our own self is no-self."

WHOEVER IS NOT AFRAID

Another quotation from the Diamond Sutra says, "If anyone listens to this discourse and is neither filled with alarm, nor awe, nor dread, be it known that such an one is of remarkable achievement." Now, of course, many people read the Diamond Sutra and do not even turn the slightest hair over it. However, they simply read the words. What this quotation is saying is that, if you've really penetrated into the meaning of the Diamond Sutra, and you are not filled with awe, dread, alarm, discouragement, fear, confusion, then you're a remarkable person. The Diamond Sutra affirms, "No wisdom can we get hold of, no highest perfection. . . ." There is no perfection, there is no ultimate attainment of being the perfect person, and there's no bodhisattva, no awakening or kensho. "In form, in feeling, will, perception, and consciousness, nowhere in them they find a place to rest on."

Nothing to rest on, nothing to cling to as a point of stability, no self. A book, *The Experience of No-Self,* tells very vividly what it means to encounter the no-self before one is ready. The author, Bernadette Roberts, says, "Everywhere I looked instead of life I saw a hideous nothing invading and strangling the life out of every object and vista in sight."[1] This anxiety may last for days, weeks, months, even years. It is one of the most formidable barriers on the way. Let it be said that because awakening is for all, regardless of whether or not one has read or even heard about Buddhism, this fear also can strike anyone regardless of their spiritual inclination or affiliation. I cannot help wondering how many people there are who are taking tranquilizers or anti-depressant medication who would be better off getting counseling from someone who has spiritual insight.

A person who has this kind of fear has seen into the truth that the Prajna Paramita, including the Diamond Sutra, is teaching: there is *no bodhisattva;* that one can save all sentient beings, but there are *no sentient beings* to save; that there is *no form* for Buddha; that the mind is indeed constantly aroused and *doesn't rest on anything.* But such a person also has not taken the final step and so feels as though he is suspended thirty thousand feet above sea level with nothing under him.

TEACHING AS A RAFT

Buddha's teaching is provisional; it is not a theory of existence; it is not a metaphysics or a system of morality. It is like a scaffolding that is put up in order that a building may be constructed. A famous saying in Buddhism, which comes out of the Diamond Sutra, is "My teaching of the good law is to be likened unto a raft. The dharma must be relinquished; how much more so the adharma." Buddha also asks in another sutra, "After you have crossed a river and arrived at the other side, would you go on carrying the raft on your head?" Thus, we can clearly see that the fundamentalist's idea of the value of the sutra is certainly not what the sutra has in mind.

RETURN TO THE KOAN

The Diamond Sutra says: "If a virtuous man or woman receives, holds in mind, reads, and recites this sutra and is scornfully reviled by others, this person has done wicked deeds in previous ages; because of this he or she falls onto hard times. Nevertheless, because of this scorn and vilification in this life, the wicked action of the former ages is thereby exhausted." The question arises that if the sutra is not simply preaching superstitious dogma, how will receiving, holding in mind, reading, and reciting help us when others revile us, and how can this recital exhaust the wicked action of the former ages? When people put us down, when we run up against injustice and are treated unfairly, how will this sutra help us?

ORIGINAL SIN

All of us have our own story of being scorned and vilified. If I ask any group of people whether they have had times of being humiliated, of being put down, of being hurt by others, each comes up with their own particular story or stories. Some of these stories may well be horrendous. Furthermore, if one reads the Psalms, one encounters again and again such expressions as "Protect me from my enemies," "Deliver me from my enemies." This is a constant theme that runs through the Psalms. In other words, a whole nation has this affliction, this scorn and vilification; after all, our enemies are people who scorn us, who put us down, run us down behind our backs. Have we then all performed some common underlying wicked act? If so, what could it be?

The Catholic Church asked itself this same question, and the answer it found was that an *original sin* had been committed. It says we are heirs to this original sin, which we make our own. Buddhism invokes something that is similar in its effect but that has quite a different origin. It says we choose our parents. This means to say we choose our life. We choose this life of suffering, and all choice ultimately has its source in our choice to be something. Furthermore, we do not choose once and for all, we are constantly making this fundamental choice, repeating it over and over again: the choice to be, the choice *to be me*. It could be said that this choice is at the root of all wicked acts: *to be is to be guilty.*

SIN AND KLESÀ

In one translation, the sutra says we have committed *wicked acts.* Other translations use the words "sins," "karmic sins," or "impure deeds." The Sanskrit word that was probably used is klesà. Let us dwell upon this word *klesà* to see how it differs from *sin* and *wicked act,* as this helps us understand the koan.

The words *wicked* and *sin* have connotations that *klesà*

does not. The word *klesà* comes from a root verb *klis*, which means "to torment," "to cause pain," "to afflict." *Sin*, on the other hand, means "to go against the dictates of God," "to disobey"; the word *wicked* was originally connected with casting a spell. The point is that with a sin we need *forgiveness*, and with a spell we need *someone* to lift the spell, whereas with *klesà* it is neither possible nor necessary for another to intervene.

A further distinction that must be made is between blame and responsibility. It is an axiom of management that one cannot delegate responsibility. This is true not only in management but in life generally. This was one of the conclusions reached at the Nuremburg trials. Although all jobs carry implicit responsibility, each person nevertheless has the responsibility for whether or not he or she will do that job. The sixth patriarch said, "When others are wrong, I too am responsible; when I am wrong, I alone am responsible." However, one can and does assign blame to others and to oneself. The tendency is to blame others for our condition. This tendency is furthered by some psychotherapies, particularly those associated with Freud. We seek in the past for what we can blame for our present woe. This search for whom to blame is making victims of us all: women are victims of men; children, of parents; patients, of doctors; and so on. From the Buddhist point of view, as we have said, the basic choice on which all else depends is the choice *to be something*. This is our responsibility, a responsibility moreover that we cannot assign to another. It is in this way that we can understand what the sixth patriarch means. In the Dhammapada it says,

> By oneself evil is done
> By oneself one suffers
> By oneself evil is undone
> No one can purify another.

CONFESSION
Both Catholic and Buddhist traditions have the ritual of confession. True confession means that one is entirely open to what one is confessing. Confession assumes complete openness and

honesty, and one must be able confess without any kind of dissimulation. It is the ultimate spiritual act, and one does not need any further absolution. Opening oneself to the responsibility, and so to be one with pain-creating situations, is an intrinsic element of the spiritual way. The difference between Christian and Buddhist confession is that Christian confession requires a priest, acting on behalf of God, to absolve the sinner from the burden of his or her sin. This is done within the context of guilt and punishment: because the sinner is guilty, he or she merits punishment, and this reasoning in turn derives from the notion of there being an ego entity, a "person," who is at fault. The punishment that is frequently given is having to recite Ave Marias a number of times, while fingering the rosary.

In Buddhism guilt comes from the choice to be something, to be *me*. Let us remember that the Diamond Sutra says, quite specifically, "No bodhisattva who is a real bodhisattva cherishes the idea of an ego entity, a personality, a being or a separated individuality." Klesá, or sins, are those actions and thoughts that I use to reinforce the choice to be an ego entity; a personality; a separate, isolated, and unique person. The feeling of guilt comes from just that separation. It is a feeling of being torn, split, sundered in one's very being. As such it is the source of all moral pain. Gurdjieff called it *Aieioiuoa*, which is the sound of a most profound groan from the heart. Therefore, instead of being punished *because* one is guilty, this torn feeling—this purgatorial pain of guilt—*is the punishment*. This in turn comes out of the claim, compounded to the detriment of others, to be something. Furthermore, the punishment inflicted by the priest, such as reciting the Ave Maria while counting the beads of the rosary, is a method used in Buddhism in order to, among other things, enable one to remain present in the midst of the purgatorial fires of guilt. In other words, it is used in quite the opposite way from how it is used in Christianity.

Zazen, it could be said, is an ongoing confessional ceremony. Instead of confessing to another, one is open to one's own true nature. One sits in the presence of one's own true nature. This could be a new way of looking at zazen. We all tend to have a commercial attitude toward practice. For a long time our practice is tainted by an egoistic demand to be the center, to achieve, to get something. This demand continues even after kensho. If one sees practice as a confession, opening oneself to the full responsibility for one's present condition, it helps undermine this commercial attitude, bringing in its wake the full realization that there is nothing to achieve, not even awakening.

Conversation with Nisargadatta

A conversation that Nisargadatta had with a questioner helps us illustrate some of what we mean. The questioner starts off by saying, "I must confess I came today in a rebellious mood. I got a raw deal at the airline's office. When faced with such situations, everything seems doubtful. Everything seems useless."

How many times have we had exactly the same feeling? We get into an argument with the clerk at the bank or with somebody who was supposed to deliver something and forgot, or we have a row with someone in the office or with the children, and we get angry about it all and then afterward say, "What's it all worth really? Nothing seems to make sense anymore." We have a feeling, "Ah gee, I don't know, I've been working all this time on myself, and it doesn't seem to make any difference at all." We start running ourselves down, running the situation down, running the world down; we doubt all that we have up till then thought worthwhile; we look for someone to blame.

Nisargadatta says, "This is a very interesting attitude. This is important to be able to doubt like that, to accept nothing, to give oneself over completely to this kind of doubting." What he wants to do is to turn the situation around. At that moment of deep despair, when we say, "Ah, God, what's the point? What good is it all to me?" we momentarily let go; we have even let go of Zen and working on ourselves. At that moment of extreme pain, when we are being dealt with unfairly, when we are angry and upset, we have let go of it all. It is at this moment of letting all go that is the ripest moment for practice, for arousing the mind without resting it upon anything.

IT IS AFTER THE FIRE OF ANGER THAT WE CAN WORK UPON IT

It so often happens that the anger flares out even before we are aware that it is rising. We strike out verbally, wounding the person in front of us. Afterward a rumination starts in which we are burning inwardly, and we desperately try to cope with this pain. Some people can ruminate on a slight for the rest of their lives. During this rumination is the time that we can start acting in a new way and allow this slight or vilification to burn like the fires of purgatory.

This is not a moral injunction; one does not do this in order to attain merit or to become a good person. This is just plain good sense. The more we can allow these purgatorial fires to burn, the more we can extirpate this root of suffering, and so, ultimately, the less suffering we're going to have to endure. It just makes perfectly good sense. It is as scientific a statement you could ever make. It does not come from mysticism, nor is it based upon morality. A moral person is one who has an image of him- or herself as good and tries to conform to this image. An ethical person, on the other hand, is one who responds naturally to the situation as a whole, which means in a way unbiased by fixed notions of what is good and bad. What the sutra is saying does, therefore, have an ethical consequence because the less this root gets in the way, the more compassion, the more openness, the more freedom, one is able to enjoy in oneself and in the presence of others, and so the more they will benefit as a consequence.

Although, as the koan says, this vilification that is visited on me was not brought about necessarily by circumstances in this present life, nevertheless, it can ameliorate the wicked actions of past lives. In other words, it is possible for us to use that experience directly to cut out this root of ego, to relinquish the choice to be separate, different, unique. When somebody does something unpleasant to you, look upon him or her as being your teacher.

I am reminded that Gurdjieff would charge people quite a lot of money to be a student of his at Fontainebleau, except for one person. Gurdjieff in fact paid this man to be there and made him supervisor over the others. He did this because this man had a natural ability to irritate other people to death. Orage, who was in his day a master of prose and a well-respected writer, was a student of Gurdjieff, and occasionally Gurdjieff would ask him to write something or other. On one occasion Orage found that Gurdjieff had given his article to another person, who was barely literate, to check "to make sure that there were no grammatical errors." Another time a woman who did the gardening for the institute, and who was very attached and proud of her garden, found that Gurdjieff had "accidentally" left open the gate so that the cows had broken in and ravaged the garden. In the Sufi tradition a teacher sometimes requires his student to deliberately break a societal rule, perhaps to steal something or make advances to a woman, with the intention of getting caught and being reviled. The student would be required to accept the consequences without giving any kind of explanation or reason.

My own feeling is that it is not necessary for us to go to these kind of extremes. Life, if we are patient, quite freely and without our asking in any way gives us our fair share of humiliation and injustice. We must, however, be ready to use it.

My Ego Is to Blame

Nisargadatta's questioner persists and says, "But the child kicks. When it is unhappy or denied anything, it kicks." Often people put themselves down in this way, and say, "I'm just like a kid, you know, there's that part of me that just takes off and squawks and squabbles and I really get identified, I get wrapped up with the situation. What good is my practice if I'm getting that wrapped up every time the neighbor looks at me in an awkward way and I fly off the handle? What good is it to me?" This is a subtle way of separating themselves from the situation. One simply becomes an observer: it is the child, the kid, who is the participant, the actor, the one who is to blame. It is like when we are at the movies and the film becomes too violent, and we say to ourselves, "It is only a movie," and withdraw our participation in the film to become simply an observer.

Nisargadatta persists and says, "Let the child kick. *Just be present at the kicking.*" (This is my emphasis.) But to be present at the kicking, we must be one with it; we have to resume responsibility, take up again the pain, be open to it. Most of us don't kick, though—we are too afraid of what people will think, and we despise ourselves for being cowardly. It is like when you are standing in front of your boss and he's just said something and you think to yourself, "Ah! Not again, this guy!" But you can't say that. You have to smile and pretend, and so you feel, "This is hypocritical, what am I? . . ." "Be present to that too," says Nisargadatta.

Going on further, Nisargadatta says, "I know that it is a painful business, but there is no remedy except one; the search for remedies must cease." Then he says the following: "If you are angry or in pain, see that you are not the pain, and then be present to the pain or anger. The physical events will go on happening, but by themselves they are not important. It is the mind alone that matters. Whatever happens, you cannot kick and scream in a bank or an airline office. Society does not allow it. If you don't like their ways or are not prepared to endure them, don't fly or carry money. Walk and if you don't want to walk, don't travel. If you deal with society, you must accept society's ways, for its ways are your ways. Your desires are so complex and contradictory—no wonder the society you create is also complex and contradictory."

We choose to carry money, we choose to fly, but beyond that, we also choose to be. Gurdjieff says choosing to be gives rise to "the need to provoke astonishment in others, bragging, cunning, the vice of eating, egoism, envy, hate, imagination, jealousy, lying, offensiveness, partiality, pride, wishing the death or weakness of others, self-conceit, self-love, swagger, vanity, slyness, ambition, double-facedness." Still we cry out for peace, for rest. "Give peace in our time, O Lord!"

Everything Is OK

True practice is a remedy because it is seeing the end of all remedies. Pure practice is the greatest hope because it is seeing the end of all hopes. Unfortunately, when the Diamond Sutra says, "There is no fundamental awakening," and later, "There is no one to awaken," we just do not take it seriously! Fundamentally, everything is OK. From the beginning all beings are Buddha. This is why the koan starts off by saying, "The Diamond Sutra says. . . ." If the koan had simply said, "If you get kicked around by people, this is the result of previous existences, and this being kicked around exhausts previous karma and so on," it would not have the same value as it has by prefacing it with "The Diamond Sutra says. . . ."

Being Present Is Not a Magic Potion

We must not believe that we've got hold of some kind of magic potion when it is said that we must become present to ourselves in difficult situations and that the difficult circumstances themselves will then go away. Many people say, "I don't understand why all of this calamity is happening to me. I've been a good person, and I have lots of faith—or at least I had a lot of faith before all this started; I'm losing my faith." In other words, being a "good person" and their "faith being present" was a talisman against the onrush of karma.

Bodhidharma

To end with, let us read from something Bodhidharma wrote that is very relevant to what we have been saying.

> If a follower of the way falls into any kind of suffering or trial, he should think and say this: During innumerable past kalpas I have abandoned the essential and followed after the accidentals, carried along on the restless waves of the sea of existence and thereby creating endless occasions for hate, ill will, and wrongdoing. Although my present suffering is not caused by any wrongdoing committed in this life, yet it is the fruit of my sins in my past existences that happens to ripen at this time. It is not

something that any men or gods could have given to me. Let me therefore take patiently and sweetly this bitter fruit of my own making without resentment or complaint against anyone. When the mind is awakened, it responds spontaneously to the dictates of reasoning so that it can make use of other people's hatred and turn it into an occasion for an advance towards the Tao.

_____

Christ said:

And when you pray, you must not be like the hyp-ocrites; for they love to stand and pray in the syna-gogues and at the street corners, that they be seen by men. Truly I say to you, they have their reward. But when you pray, go into your room and shut the door and pray to your father who is in secret; and your father who sees in secret will reward you.

_____

Dogen on Exertion

The great way of the Buddha and the patriarchs involves the highest form of exertion, which goes on unceasingly in cycles from the first dawning of religious truth, through the test of discipline and practice, to awakening and nirvana. It is sustained exertion proceeding without lapse from cycle to cycle. Accordingly, it is exertion that is neither self-imposed nor imposed by others but free and uncoerced. The merit of this exertion upholds me and upholds others. The truth is that the benefits of one's own struggles and sustained exertions are shared by all beings in the ten directions. Others may not be aware of this, and we may not realize it ourselves, but it is so. It is through the sustained exertions of the Buddhas and patriarchs that our own exertions are made possible, that we are able to reach the high road of Truth. In exactly the same way it is through our own exertions that the exertions of the Buddhas are made possible and that the Buddhas attain the high road of Truth.

This exertion too sustains the the sun, moon, and the stars; it sustains the earth and sky, body and mind, object and subject, the four elements and five *skandhas*.

The merits of these exertions are sometimes disclosed, and thus arises the dawn of religious consciousness, which is then tested in practice. Sometimes, however, these merits lie hidden and are neither seen nor heard nor realized. Yet hidden though they may be, they are still available because they suffer no diminution or restriction, whether they are visible or invisible, tangible or intangible.

At this moment a flower blossoms, a leaf falls—it is a manifestation of sustained exertion. A mirror is brightened, a mirror is broken—it is a manifestation of sustained exertion. Everything is exertion. To attempt to avoid exertion is an impossible evasion because the attempt itself is exertion. This sustained exertion is not something that people of the world naturally love or desire; yet, it is the last refuge of all.

Endnotes

Chapter 3

1. James A. Jaksa and Ernest L. Stech, *Voices from the Silence* (Toronto: Griffin House, 1980), p. 40.

Chapter 4

1. Eric Fromm, D. T. Suzuki, and Richard de Martino, *Zen Buddhism and Psychoanalysis* (London: Allen and Unwin, 1960).
2. Ibid., p. 122.
3. See, for example, Masao Abe, *Zen and Western Thought* (Honolulu: University of Hawaii Press, 1985).
4. Martin L. Gross, *The Psychological Society* (New York: Simon & Schuster, 1978), p. 9.
5. Ibid., p. 3.
6. Torrey E. Fuller, M.D. *Witch Doctors and Psychiatrists* (New York: Harper and Row, 1972), p. 32.
7. Ibid., p. 28.
8. Gross, p. 14.
9. Judson Horace Freeland, *Eighth Day of Creation* (New York: Simon & Schuster, 1979).
10. Norman O. Brown, *Life against Death* (London: Sphere Books, 1968), p. 29.
11. Gross, p. 23.
12. Ibid., p. 24.
13. Ibid.
14. They started with an MDS of 35, then dropped quickly to

15, rising to about 25 at the end of the three years. The psychotherapy patients, who took six months of treatment, had an MDS that started over 40 and never dropped below 25—an improvement that took five years. Ibid., p. 27.

15. Ibid., p. 30.
16. Eric Fromm et al., p. 137.
17. Ibid.

Chapter 6

1. *St. John of the Cross, The Dark Night of the Soul,* trans. Kurt F. Reinhardt (New York: Frederick Ungar Publishing Co., 1957), p. 40.
2. The quotations of St. John of the Cross are taken from *St. John of the Cross, The Dark Night of the Soul,* trans. Kurt F. Reinhardt (New York: Frederick Ungar Publishing Co., 1957).
3. Ibid., p. 118.
4. St. John of the Cross refers us to St. Luke xviii, 11, 12.
5. Albert Low, *The World A Gateway: Commentaries on the Mumonkan* (Boston: Charles E. Tuttle Co., Inc., 1995).
6. Mirce Eliade, *Images and Symbols,* trans. P. Mairet (London: Harvill Press, 1961), p. 5.

Chapter 14

1. Albert Low, *The Butterfly's Dream* (Boston: Charles E. Tuttle Co., Inc., 1993).

Chapter 15

1. T. S. Eliot, *The Four Quartets* (London: Faber and Faber, 1944).

Chapter 22

1. R. H. Blyth, *Haiku,* vol. 3 (Tokyo: Hokuseido Press, 1957), p. 388.
2. Ibid., p. 375.

Chapter 27

1. N. K. Sanders, trans. *Epic of Gilgamesh* (New York: Penguin, 1960), p. 196.

Chapter 28

[1] Bernadette Roberts, *The Experience of No-Self* (Boulder, CO: Shambhala, 1984).

Other Books by Albert Low

THE BUTTERFLY'S DREAM: IN SEARCH OF THE ROOTS OF ZEN
A lucid treatise on the spirituality of Zen which not only reveals the roots of Zen spirituality but shows these roots to be as much Western as they are Eastern. By so doing, the author makes Zen Accessible to Western thought and action.
5¹ᐟ² x 8¹ᐟ² 184 pages 0-8048-1822-3 paperback

AN INVITATION TO PRACTICE ZEN
There are many books on Zen, but these invariably approach the topic from a philosophical or historical perspective: one learns about Zen but not how to do Zen. This step-by-step guide is for the reader who is sufficiently intrigued by the philosophy to want to practice it. Black and white illustrations.
4¹ᐟ⁴ x 7 152 pages 0-8048-1598-4 paperback

THE IRON COW OF ZEN
Each chapter of this book begins with the discussion of a koan, a saying or action by a Zen master—perhaps the most famous is "What is the sound of one hand clapping?" Seemingly pointless or incomprehensible, the koan is actually an attempt to startle the consciousness into sudden enlightenment.
5 x 7¹ᐟ⁴ 240 pages 0-8048-1669-7 paperback

THE WORLD: A GATEWAY COMMENTARIES ON THE MUMONKAN
The *Mumonkan,* or The Gateless Barrier, is the most widely used collection of koans in Zen practice, and Albert Low, director and teacher of the Montreal Zen Centre, provides contemporary commentaries on this great collection, making it accessible to all readers and relevant to our everyday lives.
5¹ᐟ² x 8¹ᐟ² 320 pages 0-8048-3046-0 paperback

ZEN & CREATIVE MANAGEMENT
This book combines Eastern and Western thought to provide managers with a better understanding and increased awareness of themselves, their co-workers, and their company, showing how each are inter-connected.
4¹ᐟ⁴ x 7 256 pages 0-8048-1883-5 paperback

Other Books in the Tuttle Library of Enlightenment

BEYOND SANITY AND MADNESS: THE WAY OF ZEN MASTER DOGEN
by Dennis Genpo Merzel; Introduction by Maezumi Roshi
Merzel elucidates the teachings of Dogen Zenji through commentaries on three of Dogen's most significant works: Gakudo Yojinshu, Yuibutsu Yobutsu, and the Bodaisatta Shishobo.
$5^{1/2}$ x $8^{1/2}$ 304 pages 0-048-3035-5 paperback

FREE YOURSELF OF EVERYTHING: RADICAL GUIDANCE IN THE SPIRIT OF ZEN AND CHRISTIAN MYSTICISM
by Wolfgang Kopp; Translated by Barbara Wittenberg-Hasenauer
Wolfgang Kopp guides the reader step-by-step along the spiritual way, in the course of which he gives voice to the great masters of Zen and Christian mysticism through numerous vivid examples.
$5^{1/2}$ x $8^{1/2}$ 215 pages 0-8048-1989-0 paperback

FUNDAMENTALS OF MAINSTREAM BUDDHISM
by Eric Cheetham
Prepared by the distinguished Buddhist Society of London, this book aims to present the major topics of the first phase of Indian Buddhism, sometimes referred to as the Hinayana, or "the Small Vehicle." The material is drawn from major texts and commentaries, translated from the Pali and Sanskrit languages.
$5^{1/2}$ x $8^{1/2}$ 224 pages 0-8048-3008-8 paperback

GOING BEYOND BUDDHA: THE AWAKENING PRACTICE OF LISTENING
by Zen Master Dae Gak; Foreword by Zen Master Seung Sahn
This book uses a refreshingly different metaphor for Zen—that of listening. Listening can be practiced anywhere. It returns us to our true way—the way of human beings, the way of compassion.
$5^{1/2}$ x $8^{1/2}$ 256 pages 0-8048-3116-5 paperback

THE HEART OF BEING: MORAL AND ETHICAL TEACHINGS OF ZEN BUDDHISM

By John Daido Loori; Edited by Bonnie Myotai Treace and Konrad Ryushin Marchaj

Zen Master Daido Loori provides a modern interpretation of the Buddhist precepts. He presents the Buddhist teachings on a wide range of moral and social issues, taking "right action" from the monastery to the streets and homes of the modern world.

5¹/₂ x 8¹/₂ 208 pages 0-8048-3078-9 paperback

I CHING CLARIFIED: A PRACTICAL GUIDE

by Mondo Secter

This book presents the essential introductory information and hexagram commentaries required for a basic introduction and primer to the I Ching and also features an extraordinary set of specially designed cards invented by the author. Calligraphy, charts, diagrams.

5¹/₂ x 8¹/₂ 160 pages 0-8048-1802-9 paperback

THE STORY OF CHINESE ZEN

by Nan Huai-Chin; Translated by Thomas Cleary

To tell the story of Chinese Zen, Master Nan Huai-Chin, one of the world's few multi-disciplinary experts on the schools of Confucianism as well as Zen, Taoism, and esoteric Buddhism, looks to culture and history. He offers an engaging chronicle of its development and the flourishing of Chinese philosophy, arts, and literature during the Han Dynasty and earlier.

5¹/₂ x 8¹/₂ 272 pages 0-8048-3050-9 paperback

THE TAO OF ZEN

by Ray Grigg

This is the first book which systematically links Taoism and Zen. The author traces the evolution of Ch'an (Zen) in China and later in Japan, where the Way was a term used interchangeably to describe the essence of both Taoism and Zen.

5¹/₂ x 8¹/₂ 256 pages 0-8048-1988-2 paperback

TWO ARROWS MEETING IN MID-AIR: THE ZEN KOAN

by John Daido Loori

Through a comprehensive introduction and twenty-one chapters centered on koans from classic collections and modern encounters, this book presents the relevance of koan study as it relates to Zen training today.

5¹/₂ x 8¹/₂ 392 pages 0-8048-3012-6 paperback

UNDERSTANDING ZEN
by Benjamin Radcliff and Amy Radcliff
Here is the most accessible introduction to Zen yet to appear—a distinctly Western approach. Zen is explained in a simple, straightforward way, drawing analogies to the mainstream of Western science and philosophy.
$5^{1/2}$ x $8^{1/2}$ 192 pages 0-8048-1808-8 paperback

THE WHOLE WORLD IS A SINGLE FLOWER: 365 KONG-ANS FOR EVERYDAY LIFE
by Zen Master Seung Sahn; Foreword by Stephen Mitchell
"One of the most distinctive qualities of *The Whole World is A Single Flower* is its ecumenism. Dae Soen Sa Nim [Zen Master Seung Sahn] has included not only kong-ans [koans] from Chinese and Korean Zen, but also from Lao-tzu and the Christian tradition."—*Stephen Mitchell.*
$5^{1/2}$ x $8^{1/2}$ 272 pages 0-8048-1782-0 paperback

ZEN BEYOND ALL WORDS: A WESTERN ZEN MASTER'S INSTRUCTIONS
by Wolfgang Kopp; Translated by Barbara Wittenberg-Hasenauer
In the spirit of the ancient Ch'an masters, Kopp teaches a direct and powerful Zen. He conveys neither a theoretical system nor a one-sided dogmatism of sitting. Master Kopp speaks directly to the reader free of incumbencies to liberate us and lead us ultimately to the enlightenment of the mind.
53/8 x 81/2 112 pages 0-8048-3086-X paperback

ZEN LIGHT: UNCONVENTIONAL COMMENTARIES ON THE DENKOROKU
by Stefano Mui Barragato, Sensei
Bringing the varied experiences of his life and his studies in Catholicism and Quaker practice to the teachings of Zen Buddhism, the author offers off-beat, refreshing, and revealing commentaries on this Buddhist classic.
$5^{1/2}$ x $8^{1/2}$ 128 pages 0-8048-3106-8 paperback

BASIC BUDDHIST CONCEPTS
by Kogen Mizuno
This book provides lucid explanations of such fundamental concepts as the Four Noble Truths, the Eightfold Path, and the Twelve-linked Chain of Dependent Origination. Glossary-index.
$5^{1/4}$ x $8^{1/4}$ 176 pages 4-333-0123-1 paperback

Related Books from
Tuttle Publishing

THE INWARD PATH
by Nichiko Niwano
In this collection of 56 inspirational essays, the author shares his thought on what it means to live and grow as a Buddhist while carrying out one's duties amid the hurlyburly of modern city life.
4¹/⁴ x 7 168 pages 4-333-0142-0 paperback

THE LIGHT OF DISCOVERY
by Toni Packer
In this compelling collection of talks, essays, interviews, and letters, Toni Packer presents radically simple and original approaches to day-to-day living: at home, in relationships, at work, in school, in love, in grief, in therapy, and in meditation. She explores such questions as action without effort, psychotherapy, and spiritual practice, fear, the quest for enlightenment, and helping others.
6 x 9 160 pages 0-8048-3063-0 hardcover

PURE HEART, ENLIGHTENED MIND: THE ZEN JOURNAL AND
LETTERS OF MAURA SOSHIN O'HALLORAN
by Maura O' Halloran
"Most mystical experiences are almost impossible to describe, but this book comes close to conveying true Zen consciousness. [It] should become a classic in Zen literature involving Westerners." —*Library Journal*.
10 black and white line drawings. 5 x 7¹/² 192 pages
0-8048-1977-7 hardcover

WAKING FROM THE DREAM: A WEALTH OF PRACTICAL
INFORMATION RELATING TO THE BUDDHIST PATH TO
ENLIGHTENMENT
by Detong ChoYin
This lively practitioner's guide to the Buddhist path to enlightenment touches on all of the elements of Buddhist practice, from meditation and vegetarianism to the meaning of wisdom and truth.
6 x 9 320 pages 0-8048-3084-3 paperback

ZEN SEEDS: REFLECTIONS OF A FEMALE PRIEST
by Shundo Aoyama; Translated by Patricia Daien Bennage
In this fascinating collection of essays, a prominent Buddhist priest writes in plain words about the seeds of enlightenment to be found in everyday life. She explains in a clear, engaging style the nature of true happiness, the beauty radiated by a compassionate heart, and the joy offered by daily life.
4 x 7   168 pages   4-333-01478-6   paperback

For a complete catalog call or write to:
Charles E. Tuttle Co., Inc.
RR1 Box 231-5 North Clarendon, VT 05759-9700
(802) 773–6993